Funny, moving, beautiful and true to life. Ormsby captures the essence of life in a mountain village.
Lucy Abel-Smith, Author, *Travels in Transylvania* Blue Guide

Humorous affection dusts every finely-honed phrase. Rare insights couple with delightful depictions in these charming stories. Ormsby's turn of phrase exerts a gentle but persistent grip and reveals a Transylvania even more beguiling than we suspected.
Douglas Williams, Editor, *OZB magazine*

Each story throws open another window onto life in Romania, filtered through Ormsby's warm and witty humour. Alternating between the absurd, the surreal, the comic, the tragic and the profound – and often combining all – this is a journey through the everyday triumphs, frustrations and revelations of a foreigner in his adopted country. The book is as varied and surprising as Romania itself. The writing is taut, with no words wasted. Affectionate, entertaining and very funny.
Nick Hunt, Author, *Walking the Woods and the Water*

Step into Transylvania with Mike Ormsby as your personal guide, complete with his knowledge, keen eyes and ears, and distinctive humour. He conjures scenes with a lovely light touch; you'll be right there, as I was.
Nigel Shakespear, Editor, *Times New Romanian*

Mike Ormsby's stories are like 65 proof palinca offered to you at 10 a.m. They fill you with happiness and sadness, at the same time.
Raluca Feher, Author, *America dezgolită de la brâu în jos*

A colourful picture of people, their lifestyle, and customs, painted by an Englishman with an exceptional sense of humour. Welcome to Palincashire!
Ruxandra Biro, Reference Librarian, Cluj County Library

Ormsby is as close to understanding the fascinating nature of Romanians as are the wisest of our fellow countrymen.
Claudia Craiu, Journalist, Task Force Media

© 2017, Mike Ormsby   *Ormsbymike*   *mikeormsby.net*
© 2017, Nicoaro Books   *NicoaroBooks*   *nicoarobooks.com*

All rights reserved. No part of this publication may be reproduced, or transmitted in any form or by any means, electronic or otherwise, without written permission from the author.

ISBN print edition: 978-606-93902-8-3
ISBN create space edition: 978-1973896197

Cover design by Sorin Sorasan   *sorinsorasan.com*
DTP by Victor Jalbă-Șoimaru   *prodtp.ro*
Author photo by Cosmin Bumbuț

Descrierea CIP a Bibliotecii Naționale a României
  ORMSBY, MIKE
  Palincashire: Tales from Transylvania /
  Mike Ormsby. – București: Nicoaro Books, 2017
  ISBN: 978-606-93902-8-3

821.111

PALINCASHIRE
TALES OF TRANSYLVANIA

MIKE ORMSBY

Table of Contents

Acknowledgements 9

The Magic Words 17
Infectious Pizza 22
I Spy 28
Black Van 38
Man with a Plan 45
How to cure Chickenpox 57
Love Thy Neighbour 62
Palincashire 70
Uncle Nelu 89
Marvellous Market 96
Run for Your Life 102
No Business like Snow Business 105
Tango's Foxtrot 121
Back in Five 133
Hrrrnnnh! 154
Tyranny 162
Keep the Home Fires Burning 170
Dog for a Dog 179
We Are Not Alone 191
Finding Solomon 202
Someone Else 208
Solomon the Wise Guy 214
One Way 219

Author Bio 227

These stories have been twice distilled
in our oak-lined library.

Acknowledgements

Thank you, Angela Nicoară, for editing and insight.

Thank you, Emanuela Jalbă-Șoimaru
and Carmen Stanilă, for proofreading. Typos are
inevitable, but I'm grateful for your thyme.

Thank you, friends and neighbours in Transylvania,
Romania, for sharing your wit, wisdom, and palinca.

Mike Ormsby
Transylvania
7.7.17

For Romanians and Romaniaphiles everywhere

The wind is low, the birds will sing
That you are part of everything.

John Lennon & Paul McCartney

I first heard about Palincashire from my friend Andy Hockley. Located in Transylvania, central Romania, this magical land will delight and challenge even the most intrepid visitor. If you can find Palincashire on a map, don't buy it.

The Magic Words

The elderly woman standing in the centre of Brașov has sad eyes and a big book: *The Brothers Grimm.* She looks about as hungry as the wolf on the cover. She offers the book to some passers-by, who pass but don't buy. She spots me approaching and says, "Mister, Mister, twenty lei."

Twenty lei. That's what, about five euros? I pause for a peep, flicking musty pages. It's a vintage hardback in Romanian with good illustrations, and she needs the cash. Her floral dress is washed out and an empty shopping bag dangles from her wrist. It's no fairy tale out here under this scorching summer sun.

"Call it fifteen lei, Mister, if you like."

I open my wallet and pay up. "Done."

"Mulțumesc, God bless."

She has good manners and I have *Hansel & Gretel.* Not to mention all the rest. I'll read some on the train home, improve my vocabulary. What's *gingerbread* in Romanian?

I hop on a bus for the station, gazing out at the cobbled lanes and tall, narrow houses with their solid beams and steep roofs. Like so much of Transylvania, this place offers tantalising hints of history.

The bus cruises around a slow bend and I gaze at the huge, steep, wooded hill overlooking the city. The Dacians dug a bone pit on that hill – evidence of a pagan cult, according to the archeologists – and, once upon an empire, somewhere up that slope, the Romans built a sacrificial altar dedicated to the god Tempus – their personification of *the moment* or *a convenient opportunity*. That's why, these days, that hill is called *Tâmpa,* although you should probably check, because times change and it might be called *Rolex* by now.

German colonists had their opportunity in the 12th century, when Hungarian kings invited them to build, mine and cultivate; they came, saw, and Saxonized this region, followed by the Teutonic Knights who founded the city during the Crusades, called it *Kronstadt,* and lost it when the Hungarians booted them out. Eventually, the communists turned up, whose genius, lest we forget, paved the way for McDonalds, Pizza Hut, and Starbucks. Three hundred years from now, perhaps little green men and lanky purple women will stroll through these narrow alleys with the thick walls and low arches, and wonder what was in our burgers. Interesting place, Brașov. Winter can be hard in the Carpathian Mountains, but, so far, this summer seems just right.

The station is as decrepit as ever, although the trains run on time, sometimes. *Platform 1 in 10 minutes* can mean *Platform 4 in 2 minutes,* and *A forty-minute delay* can mean *You should've brought your sleeping bag.* Assuming, of course, that you can fathom the travel updates bawled from tannoy speakers in this humungous hall of unintelligible echoes. It's like standing in a salt mine, where all you can find is pepper.

I doubt the ancient Romans would put up with it, if they were here. They'd sacrifice that travel announcer, on their altar, for telling whoppers. Then again, looking on the bright side, all this would probably make a good PR campaign: *Free Fairy Tale with Every Ticket.*

I buy mine from a large woman who lives in a small kiosk, then walk up pink marble stairs to the mezzanine – a good place to wait. I find an unbroken plastic seat, and sit. Dusty hikers trudge past. A middle-aged man in a Ceaușescu-era safari suit squints at the schedule. A pee-stained drunk lies face up, on a bench, mouth open. *What if one of these soaring pigeons plops in it?*

A pretty girl in a tatty yellow T-shirt trots towards me. She's about eight years old. Her jeans are too big and her long belt is looped twice around her concave tummy. She smiles, head tilted.

"Mister, give me money."

It seems this is my job and she's my boss. I smile back. "Hello there, and what are the magic words?"

"Huh?"

I explain about *please.* "The magic words are *vă rog.*"

"*Vă rog,* Mister."

I hand her two lei. "And afterwards?"

She grins, cute little beggar that she is. *"Vă rog,* Mister."

"No, *mulțumesc.*"

"*Mulțumesc.*"

She skips away but soon returns, chewing a sticky bun as big as her head. She sits nearby, *munch munch,* smiling. She knows a sucker when she sees one. I'm an ATM on legs. She has big brown eyes. I glimpse a bright future in there and beckon her. *You, here, now.* She approaches with a wary gaze.

"What's your name, please?" I ask.

"Rushinta."

"I'm Mike. Can you read?"

"Sigur, domnu'!"

"Glad to hear it, this is for you."

I pull *The Brothers Grimm* from my bag and Rushinta's eyes pop when she clocks the dastardly wolf. "This is for me?"

"Yes, and I want to write your name inside. How do I spell it?" I dip in my bag for a pen.

Rushinta has other ideas. "Let me do it!" She sits alongside. "Big letters or small ones?"

"As you wish."

I give her the pen and she writes her name, slowly, in block capitals on the flyleaf. I scribble a dedication underneath and she grabs her prize. "Should I read this book now?"

"If you like, Rushinta."

She runs a finger across the first page, mouthing the words. After a few minutes, she looks up. "Ten lines already, Mister."

"Congratulations. Any good, that story?"

"Yes, but why did you give me this book?" Rushinta wrinkles her little nose at me. Strangers don't give you books. They give you money, or food, or nothing. I sit wondering. *Ah, I know.* I pull my keys from a pocket and select one at random. "This is a key to a door, Rushinta."

She looks at the key, then at me. "I know."

I point at her page. Her fingertip is poised, so I'd better be brief. "Rushinta, books are important. They are the key to your future, they will open doors in your life. Do you understand?"

"Sort of."

"Good, so read every day. You'll get smarter, every day, I promise. Do you promise?"

She sighs and looks a bit worried. *Every day?* Perhaps time is tight at home. "I'll try."

"Good, please do. Now, how are Hansel and Gretel doing?"

Rushinta reads aloud and I listen, watching pigeons soar. What were the chances, today, that I'd meet a tired old woman who needed money and an energetic little girl who needs something more? All I need now is a pigeon to plop in that drunk's gob. *Vă rog.*

I sit in my train, watching people shuffle along the platform with their bags and worried faces. A sweaty guard taps the steel wheels with a steel rod. Question is why.

A yellow blur rouses me. Rushinta zigzags between the travellers, begging here, pleading there. Most ignore her but some oblige with cash. She's not carrying the book. Perhaps she sold it. *Binned it?* She slithers through a group of hikers and vanishes from my sight. Never mind. I'll watch the sweaty guard.

Rushinta reappears soon enough, perched on a bench and kicking her heels. She doesn't see me. A whistle blows, wheels turn, and my train clanks away. I doubt we'll meet again. She'll forget our chat. Just another weird foreigner. One who can't help but watch and wonder from his seat.

Rushinta twists around, tugging at something tucked under her belt. She pulls the book free, lays it on her lap, and opens the cover. She turns the pages carefully and places a finger. Her little feet stop swinging as she reads the magic words.

Infectious Pizza

The cat flap flaps. A little furry head pokes through it, from the dark night beyond into our house. Bright green eyes glance left and right. Long whiskers sprout from the smudgy, black and white face. Freddie is not what you'd call a beautiful puss, but he's got something. Cattitude, that's what. *Here comes trouble.*

Tonight, he's also got something in his jaws: a tiny mouse alive and wriggling. But not for much longer, unless I intervene. Freddie realises that he's being watched and glares back at me with contracted pupils, two slits of suspicion. *Stay away, you.*

Some people might claim that a cat brings home a mouse as a gift for the master. *Really?* Try telling the cat.

Freddie scuttles under a chair and emits a strange noise, more growl than meow. I kneel and reach under.

"May I have that?"

Freddie makes another strange noise. *Fuck off.*

"Charming. Have you forgotten who rescued you?"

I never asked to be rescued.

"What if I drag you out, kitten mitten?"

You can try. Still mine.

"Actually, that mouse is a gift for me. Or so the experts say. You should read more, Fred."

You should mind your own business.

I tug our cat from his refuge and press my fingers gently at the hinge of his jaw. He drops the mouse. It darts under a rug. Freddie licks his pride and shoots me a glittering glance. *Thanks a lot.*

Now it's my turn to hunt, with an old spatula and a deep plastic box. Freddie watches with disdain. *Amateur.* But soon enough, the mouse scampers into the box, round and round, up and down, its tiny pink paws grappling in vain for traction. Seems in excellent shape too, considering its recent ordeal.

"There's a lucky rodent. Ye shall be released."

Freddie stares at me. *WTF?*

The mouse rises on its haunches, all whiskers and twitchy nose, to eye me up. I think we're bonding. It senses freedom is imminent, yay. I'm equally pleased. We're friends, now. I reach into the box, scoop up my cute little captive, and head for the door. A warm, evening breeze wafts in my face. Life is good.

The mouse jiggles in my hands. It needs air, perhaps. I open a gap between my interlocked thumbs and a grey head pokes though it. Tiny black eyes glisten, shiny as caviar. We observe each other – man and mouse – in wonder and mutual respect. Then it bites my thumb. *Take that.* I yelp in pain and drop the vicious little bastard, before it chews my arm off. Freddie rushes to reclaim his prize, flipping the mouse left and right. It is soon dazed, confused, and back in his jaws. Freddie slinks sway. *The End.*

I slump in a chair to inspect the damage. Fascinating stuff, blood. How it catches the light, shines ruby, regulates the life in us and scares the life out of us. My scarlet blob is growing bigger by the heartbeat. *What now?*

I'll probably bleed to death, home alone up this mountain. Or develop rabies and bounce off the walls at the sight of dishwater. What a way to go. I should probably write my will before my sacred ink runs out. Actually, I have a better idea. *Phone the vet.* He'll know what to do.

Cosmin takes my call but sounds weary – and who wouldn't – after a long day tending poorly animals. I explain that I have been most cruelly served by an ungrateful mouse. After a short silence, Cosmin says, "Mike, what are you, fucking nuts?"

In medical school, this is known as bedside manner, but then again, Cosmin didn't go there. He went to a school for veterinarians, if that's how you spell it.

We discuss the likelihood of my untimely demise from bubonic plague, and so on. It seems the risks are negligible but you never know. Cosmin asks when I last had a tetanus jab, but I never know. "I've had a yellow fever jab, Cosmin, is that any good?"

"Mike, don't you know anything?"

"If I drive down, can you give me a tetanus jab?"

"I'm a vet, not a doctor. You should go to Brașov and find the Hospital for Infectious Diseases."

"Oh, great, at this hour? Where is it, anyway?"

"In Brașov. Just ask for *Spitalul de Boli Infecțioase.* Write it down, in case you forget. Was it a mouse, or a baby rat?"

"I didn't ask. How does a baby rat look?"

"Like a rat."

"It was a mouse."

"Well, you should still go to the hospital."

Go to the hospital? I peer at my thumb. The bleeding has stopped. Perhaps I'll survive the night. Besides, *Brașov?*

"Cosmin, that's eighty kilometres. In the dark."

"You don't have headlights?"

"They're a bit wonky. Can I go tomorrow?"

"Up to you. Depends how long you want to live."

"Perhaps we should say goodbye."

So we do, and I reach for my car keys. Walking towards the door, I step on something tiny, furry, and dead. It's my bloody attacker, I'd know that face anywhere. Freddie sits nearby, licking his paws and doing the washing up – ears first, of course.

The dark and twisting forest road is dark and twisting even in daylight, but at night, with drunken headlights, it's enough to make you ratty. I could kill that rodent if it wasn't dead. Next time a cat brings me a present, I'll make popcorn. *Showtime.*

On we go. This rattling Suzuki jeep was modified for off-road shenanigans, but not by me. The drive takes an hour and by 11 p.m., I spy the twinkling, ancient city of Brașov. Sleeker cars zoom past me, containing lucky people who'll live long and happy lives if they slow down. Where are they off to, at this ungodly hour? Shouldn't they be home watching shite on Romanian TV? Look at them go, probably got Sat Nav, as well, whereas I have a scrap of paper bearing feverish scrawl – *Boli Infecțioase.* Infectious Diseases. *I've probably got one.* I need the hospital and soon. I hope it's open. Damn that mouse. I'd better get better directions if I want to get better. Time is slipping away.

I park outside an all-night pharmacy, pop inside, and explain that I've been bitten by a huge rat with teeth like this – *NEH-NEH-NEH* – and that I need the wotsit hospital. A handsome lady in a lab coat points up the street: *left, right, left again.* Her silver-haired male colleague peeps from a room behind her and looks me up and down. The fever is kicking in. He can tell.

After fifteen minutes of driving in circles, triangles, and rectangles, I realise I'm lost, literally and metaphorically. Not to mention scientifically, since I'll surely be dead by dawn. But how come? I've asked three people thus far, so either I'm hallucinating or they gave me dicky directions. *Ah, look, some zombies at a bus stop; one of them will know.* I park nearby and stride back to ask my question, but I've forgotten how to say *hospital*. Hmm, I'll say it like the French and omit the <s> in the middle: *hopital.* That should do it. The people at the bus stop turn to listen, as I approach and ask:

"Hôpital de boli infecțioase, vă rog?"

They seem a bit lost, which makes six of us.

"Domnul," says the woman nearest, "we don't live round here. Try that driver in the pizza van."

She points and I turn. Great idea. The pizza man is sitting with his window rolled down, fiddling with his keys. He starts the car, just as I glide up.

"Hôpital de boli infecțioase, vă rog?"

He raises bushy eyebrows. "*What* kind of pizza?"

We stare at each other in mutual wonder, but not much respect. He drives off before I can ask again. I have a feeling that something got lost in translation. Me, actually. None the wiser, I slink back to my car, raising a throbbing thumb at the bus queue. *All sorted, cheers.*

Eventually, I find the hospital – a small, nondescript building behind tall trees in a quiet street. No neon, no gates, no nothing, really. Blink and you'd miss it. Even so, I'm blinking relieved to be here.

The helpful young doctor listens carefully and summons a nurse, who prepares an injection and asks what sort of rodent bit me. I pull a transparent plastic zip-lock bag from my pocket. "This sort."

The nurse takes a step back. "Is that a mouse?"

"Hope so. It's dead, don't worry. Freddie killed it. He's my cat."

The doctor asks me to put the bag on a bench, out of harm's way. He sticks the needle in my arm and offers advice about what to do next time Freddie catches a mouse. Or rather, what not to do. His pager beeps, he bids me farewell and departs.

The nurse puts a little plaster on my arm. "You should be fine, but if not, just phone. Will that be all, or is there anything else, Domnul?"

Her perfume smells of roses and she has a lovely, reassuring smile. I do like nurses and rather wish I was a bit more sick. Oh, well. No, wait, I know.

"Actually, Nurse, please could you tell me how to pronounce the name of this place, in Romanian?"

"*Spitalul de Boli Infecțioase.*" She sounds proud, probably because it sounds so impressive, unlike whenever I say it. No wonder I got lost. But now I'm found. I will drive through the valley of darkness, with wonky headlights, fearing no evil.

"You've been very helpful, Nurse, *mulțumesc și la revedere.*"

"Don't forget your mouse," she says, pointing to the little plastic bag.

I Spy

After a half-hour hike along a dirt road of muddy puddles, treacherous potholes, and darting deer that send our dogs delirious, Angela and I reach one of our favourite spots – a gentle hill on the southern edge of Culmea with spectacular views of soaring mountains. Far below us, neighbouring villages nestle in a wide valley flanked by wooded slopes. White clouds balloon across an azure sky.

We rest with our gasping companions – Linda the Rottweiler cross, and Sam the long-eared, wannabe Husky. We have two more friends with us today – our seven-year-old neighbour Dragoș is tagging along his rather large sheepdog pup Ursulică.

Dragoș is a good-looking lad with a cowlick and irresistible grin; Ursulică is of the Mioritic or *barac* breed – all fluff and fun. He looks like an Old English Sheepdog – shaggy white coat, loping gait, and eyes that glint like coal. *Ursulică* means *Little Bear,* and he might have to chase big ones when he grows up.

We sit among tall haystacks, breathing easy. The dogs lounge about, competing for our caresses, growling but not really. I'm chewing on a stalk of sweet grass and gazing at distant hills – wave after wave of green.

I could be sitting on the bridge of a mighty ship. It's blissfully quiet on this ocean of rural calm, but not for long. Dragoș peeps at me from under his *New York Yankees* cap. Yesterday, it was a *Laser Quest* cap. He's got a big collection.

"Domnul Mike, shall I start?"

I give him the nod and Angela casts me a knowing smile because the real question is whether Dragoș will ever stop. He puffs up his chest, squinting into the distance. "I spy, with my–"

He seems to have run out of things to spy. Hardly surprising, as we play this game several times a week. He points at the dogs. They sit erect, heads cocked and radars locked on. *To what?*

"Deer coming," says Dragoș.

We wrap the dogs' leashes tightly around our wrists, just in case. After a few tense moments, we hear pitiful mewling. It's the sound of tiny animals in distress and getting louder by the second.

"Pups," says Angela.

"Kittens, I reckon."

"Pups, Mike. I know that sound from when I was a kid. Our neighbour took a sack of pups to the salty lake. We didn't ask why."

A warm breeze carries the incessant squeals up our hill but from where? Angela points.

"Down there, that lady, see? She's got them, I bet."

A spindly figure scurries along the road thirty metres below us, at the base of our hill. She's wearing dark clothes and a floppy beige sun hat. A white plastic sack dangles from her forearm.

"She's going to kill them." Angela rises to her feet, cups a hand to her mouth, and yells, "Excuse me, Doamna!"

The woman quickens her pace without so much as a glance in our direction. Deaf as a post with no time to lose, I reckon.

"Think she heard you, Angela?"

"She heard me, that's why she's hurrying, look at her go."

The woman scoots along, transferring the sack to her other arm, out of sight. Angela shouts again, "Doamna! Where are–"

The woman disappears behind a copse of silver birch, where the road bends, and we receive no answer, except from the birds and bugs. Angela and I lock eyes. *Now what?* I glance at little Dragoş, who shrugs, equally bemused. Then we all start downhill, pulled by our three panting dogs who knew, long before we did, that something was wrong. Perhaps together, we can put it right.

By the time we reach the birch trees, the woman is nowhere to be seen, which is odd considering this road stretches straight ahead for half a kilometre before the next bend. *Where is she?*

"Probably in the forest," says Angela.

We scan a thousand trees to our left and right. Hopeless task. She's gone. We'll never find her. I suppose we could release the dogs to track the squeals, but they'll probably scent a cat instead and bugger off for an hour to bark up the wrong bark.

An engine rumbles and we turn to see a familiar yellow pick-up truck trundling towards us along the road. Our pretty young neighbour Mirela is driving it; her husband Tudor is in the passenger seat and waving a bare arm at us, as they slow down for a chat.

"Hello there, Doamna Angela. Out for a walk?" A thick gold chain hangs around Tudor's bull neck and his cute toddler son Mihăiță is balanced precariously on daddy's knee.

"Nice day for it," says Mirela. She has a lovely smile and no safety belt, despite the perilous road. In fact, neither of them does. *And where's the infant chair? What if they hit a bad bump or slide into a ditch?* Tiny Mihăiță will smash into the windscreen, possibly even through it. I'm tempted to mention this, but desist because they'd just laugh. Only fools wear safety belts.

Tudor's teenaged son Tudorel leans from the rear seat. "Is everything oκ, Domnul Mike?"

"Not really." I explain about the sack of squealing pups, and he grins. *Yeah, it happens.* It seems pointless to say any more, but I rest my hand on the roof of their truck and try again. "So, folks, if you see a woman with a white sack, somewhere along this road, please talk to her about it."

Tudor sits fingering his gold chain. "And say what?"

It's a good question and I'm still wondering how to answer it when they drive away. *See ya.*

Angela, Dragoș, and I continue along the dirt road with our dogs. The woman with the squealing sack has vanished into thin air. Or thick forest. But we're keeping an eye out, just in case.

"Actually, I know who it was," says Angela, "I gave her a lift last summer. *Anamaria?* No, but something like that. She wanted a ride to that little chapel in the village, she's one of those reborn Christians."

"Born again?"

"Yes, and she's from one of the oldest families around here, or so she said. They have lots of land, a big guesthouse, and a nice car. She seemed nice enough. Oh, wait, now I remember. *Aneta,* yes, that's her, Doamna Aneta, a widow. She even invited me to her chapel, very pious, she was."

"Maybe she's taking her puppies to get baptised."

"Not funny, Mike. She'll leave them in the forest, I bet."

"Already did, Angela. I spy with my little eye, look."

I point along the road, as The Incredible Vanishing Woman emerges from the trees, empty-handed. She strides towards us in dusty tennis shoes, swinging her long arms ever so gracefully. Her baggy cardigan is wrinkled and her black linen pants are faded, but she got style for her age and exudes a certain rustic elegance, glamour even. I picture her in a romantic movie about mature love in the mountains, with Vivaldi as soundtrack. *The Four Seasons,* starring Doamna Aneta.

She breezes past us with a brief nod and a careful cough, as you do. Close up, she looks about seventy-five years old, possibly eighty. She's stick thin with a healthy complexion and pale brown eyes. Probably quite a beauty in her day, but that was then.

Angela gets straight to it. "Doamna Aneta, where are they?"

"Sorry?" Aneta places a palm on her chest – perish the thought, and so on. Actually, forget Hollywood; she's no actress.

"You had a sack of puppies, Doamna Aneta, where is it?"

"Oh, that?"

"Yes, that."

"Hmm, well, I left it in the forest."

"Where a bear or a fox will eat those puppies alive?"

Aneta shrugs her spindly shoulders. "What else can I do?"

"You could sterilise your dog, for a start."

"With what money?"

Angela counts Aneta's alleged riches, on splayed fingers. "You have a guesthouse, cows, sheep, and many acres of land. Please, Aneta, don't pretend you can't afford twenty-five euros?"

"I can't."

"Really? I've seen a nice Range Rover in your yard."

"Not for a while, you haven't." Aneta sighs, and looks around as if wondering how much more she should or shouldn't tell us. "That car belonged to a tourist who stopped visiting. I closed down my guest house, if you must know. As for land, I'm trying to sell it but nobody is buying, and the same goes for the milk and cheese. I have hardly any money. My so-called pension is pitiful. Yesterday, my dog had seven pups. I've kept two but I can't afford to feed the rest."

"You can't just dump them," I say.

Aneta purses her lips. "Well, I did, so there."

I play my ace. "Surely you know that God sees everything?"

Pretty rich coming from an atheist, but all is fair in love and paw. Aneta turns her glassy gaze on me. I'm expecting a telling-off, but she doesn't seem angry, just lost, a lady beaten by the march of time. I feel sorry for her, but not much. Ladies don't dump puppies.

Aneta spreads her hands. "Domnul, believe it or not, I love animals. I have a calf that I cannot bring myself to kill, although I could easily sell the meat. I have a bull, same thing. I have four cats, three dogs, and hardly a

33

bean to eat. Yes, it's wrong, what I did today, but at least they could not see me. It's easier, that way."

"Who could not see you?"

"The puppies. Their eyes were not yet open when I put them in the forest. Yes, it's bad, but as I said, what can I do?"

I have no answer, only a request. "Show us where, please?"

Doamna Aneta points. "Back there, through the gap."

Dragged by our dogs, Angela, Dragoş and I stride along the road and into the forest. We pause to listen. Not a sound. A clammy darkness looms, penetrated by flickering sunbeams. Aneta calls instructions from the edge of the road. "Lower, at the rocks."

Linda seems to understand. She's in four-wheel dog mode and hauls me down the slope. I slide on my haunches, dislodging stones, and cracking dry twigs. Linda stops to listen. I crouch beside her. I can hear squealing. *From the left?* Linda lunges to the right, all muscle, towards a rocky ledge where bags of rubbish, cigarette packets, and squashed beer cans lie around the remains of a long-abandoned campfire. A knotted white sack wobbles among the detritus. *They're still alive.*

"Mike?" Angela's voice filters from above. "You ок?"

I grab the wriggling sack and clamber back up towards the dappling light. "I'm fine. Found the pups. Well, Linda did."

Back at the roadside, we untie the shiny white sack and peep inside. Tiny snouts twitch at us and minuscule paws claw the air. The five blind pups are silky black and no bigger than moles, but their pitiful wails could wake the dead.

"These little ones should be with their mother," says Angela.

Aneta nods and seems almost relieved, somehow. I start to retie the neck of the sack but she intervenes with a bony hand. "No, Domnul, they'll suffocate."

I cradle the sack in my arms. Aneta sighs, shaking her head, but not at me. It feels like progress. We are no longer adversaries embroiled in a problem but colleagues seeking its solution. Angela explains that we just want to help, and how. Aneta listens hard and agrees to let the puppies wean for a few more weeks back home.

"And afterwards?" Aneta's mouth twists in doubt. *Your move, folks*.

We assure her that things will work out, because we'll post photos of the pups on Facebook and people are sure to want them.

"Which *people?*" says Aneta, "I'm not giving these to just anyone. Fine dogs, they'll be, one day. Not mutts, trust me. Give them here, please."

I pass her the wriggling sack. Trust is all. The mood between us is hardly friendly, but we've reached an understanding. She carries the sack carefully, keeping it close to her chest and cooing gentle words as she goes. We follow at a respectful distance, walking three abreast as if mourning the dead. Or perhaps we're quietly celebrating the rebirth of compassion.

Dragoș nudges my arm and speaks from the side of his rosebud mouth. "Domnul Mike? Those puppies were not born yesterday, like Doamna Aneta told you. They were born today, a few hours ago."

I drape an arm over his shoulder. "And how can you tell?"

"It's easy. They were all wet when you opened the sack. If they had been born *yesterday,* the mummy dog should have licked them all over, by now. They would be clean and dry. Not wet."

"You're a smart lad, Dragoș."

"Mulțumesc."

"Not born yesterday, indeed," says Angela.

"Domnul Mike?"

"Yes, Dragoș?"

"Are we going home?"

"After we go to Doamna Aneta's house to finalise things."

"What does that mean?"

"Good question."

Aneta's house is clad in stout logs and sits amid a buzzing orchard at the end of a white gravel path. Sheep graze and gaze as we approach the front gate. It looks a nice, cosy place. Perhaps we'll get a cup of tea. Then again, maybe not. Doamna Aneta opens the gate and closes it behind her, to nip any big buddy ideas in the bud.

Instead, we chat over the fence with her wary-looking, middle-aged son Dinu, who sports a goatee beard, a sorry sweater, and rubber clogs with gaping holes. I spy his socks; hand-knitted woollen socks, probably itchy. "Sterilisation?" Dinu sounds anxious, as if we meant for him.

"It's the best solution," says Angela.

"Besides, they've offered to contribute," adds Doamna Aneta.

She places the white sack in their yard and disappears into the house. Perhaps she's gone to put the kettle on. The sack jiggles left and right. The five pups inside are shrieking for their mummy's milk. It's an unholy din, and a small brown dog with large teats comes to investigate, yipping and pawing. She seems somewhat demented and so would you, if your howling offspring were tied in a sack. Angela points a finger. "Aren't you going to let them out, Domnul?"

"Soon," says Dinu. "So, how much can you contribute?"

"We'll pay for the sterilisations," says Angela.

"And bring food, when the pups are old enough," I suggest.

"Generous," says Dinu, "but we can't let you pay for it all."

"Fair enough, how much can you contribute?" I ask.

Dinu tugs his beard. It looks almost glued on. "Ten euros."

"You mean per pup, or in total?"

"Per pup, we're not that poor."

"It's a deal," says Angela.

We shake hands with Dinu but there's no sign of Aneta. She's probably having a lie down, exhausted from all that rescuing.

"And thanks, by the way," says Dinu. "Want some cheese?"

Strolling home, we pause to pluck luscious raspberries from the hedgerows and they taste great with nibbles of Dinu's salted *brânza*. Linda, Sam, and Ursulică sit on their haunches like good doggies waiting for their share. Dragoș pushes back the peak of his baseball cap and looks around. "Domnul Mike?"

"Yes, Dragoș."

"Shall I start?"

We give him the nod, because it's time for some fun.

Black Van

Our young neighbour Dragoș stands in the lane outside our house, clutching a big plastic bottle full of milk. No smile today. He looks a bit worried, as if he's forgotten something. The sunset casts a long shadow behind him. He peeps through the fence at me. "You're playing a guitar, Domnul Mike."

"I am indeed. It's nice to sit out here. Are you ok, Dragoș?"

He nods, somewhat unconvincingly, and holds up the bottle. "For you."

"I was hoping you might say that." I set my guitar aside, rise from the rough wooden bench, and walk to unlock the gate.

Dragoș steps into our yard and gives me the bottle. It contains two litres of creamy, pale yellow milk, still warm from the cow. You could not wish for better. This stuff should be in Harrods' Food Hall, selling for top dollar. "Thank you, Dragoș."

"Cu plăcere."

Our dog Linda trots up, expecting a pat on the head from our neighbour, but Dragoș just sucks his lower lip, preoccupied.

Angela appears in the doorway. I pass her the bottle and she carries it into the house. *"Mulțumesc,* Dragoș. Two minutes?"

"Bine, Doamna Angela."

We sit on the bench, side by side. My favourite place, this, especially on a warm evening. A nice spot to bask in the last rays of the sun and listen to buzzing bugs, and shepherds beating kinks out of their scythes. We watch six men, on the opposite hill, squatting in a little circle with their hammers going up and down. *Tap-tap-tap.* I hope they don't cut their thumbs like Certain People did.

"How are your cows, Dragoș?"

"Bine, mulțumesc."

"And your dogs?"

"Bine."

"What's up?"

He shrugs. "Nothing, Domnul Mike, why?"

"You seem worried."

"Me?"

"Yes, are you worried?"

Dragoș looks away. He's worried, all right.

Angela reappears on the steps of the house and gives him a little parcel of greaseproof paper, all folded and tucked. Dragoș brightens up a bit. "What's this, Doamna Angela?"

"Banana cake for your mum."

"Mulțumesc."

"My pleasure. When is your dad back from Italy?"

Dragoș shrugs. "I'd better get home. Bye, then."

I open the gate to let him out. Clutching his parcel, he steps into the lane. "And if you see a black van, you must call the police."

"A black van?" says Angela.

Dragoş nods, glancing left and right. He seems ready to weep. "A black van with black windows. They drive it around here."

"Who does?" I ask.

"Some men, Domnul Mike. They offer you sweets. Then, they grab you and put you in the van. They cut you open with a big sharp knife. They steal your insides and sell them. Then you die."

"What?" says Angela, "who on earth told you all that?"

"It was on the news. *Organ snatchers* is what they're called."

"Organ snatchers?"

"In a black van with black windows. Did you see it, Doamna?"

"No, Dragoş, and you shouldn't worry. Really, I don't think any of that is true. I doubt that we have organ snatchers in Culmea."

"It's true, Doamna Angela. It was on television, on the news."

"You saw this, Dragoş?" I ask.

"No, Domnul Mike, but someone did."

"Who?"

"Someone in my class. Kids are disappearing."

"Kids from our village?"

"I'd better go." Dragoş strides away. Breaks into a trot. Home is only a hundred yards away, but even so. He runs down the twisting lane. Gone. Kids are disappearing.

"Poor lad has some weird ideas," says Angela.

"Same last summer. The missing aircraft, remember?"

"Vaguely, yes. Something about a big jet?"

"Boeing 747 crashed into a bus queue in Brașov. *Sixty-three people dead,* Dragoș told me."

"But in reality?"

"A two-seater glider crashed in the mountains."

"That, I do remember. I'd better go and boil this milk."

"I'll stay out here for a bit. And watch for a black van."

"With black windows."

Angela goes back into the house and I reach for my guitar, but the moment is gone and I don't feel like strumming. I can still see Dragoș's little face. He looked petrified, poor lad.

Where do such stories come from? How do the facts and fables of the international organ network filter into the impressionable mind of a six-year-old boy in the mountains of Transylvania? Talk about a global village. I'll Google it, later, see what I find.

Linda nuzzles her wet nose into my hand. I stroke her silky ears and gaze at green hills. The tapping has stopped and the burly shepherds on the next hill have resumed cutting the grass.

I watch them working in a row, strung out across the field, six men side-by-side, about two metres apart. They advance at the same speed, swinging their scythes back and forth. Looks easy but takes years of practise. They've probably done it every summer since they were teenagers and can shave an acre before you can say, *My back hurts.* They'll work late, as every evening, slicing grass into neat lines, pausing only to sharpen or beat their blades, and take a brief swig from a bottle of water or beer.

Idyllic, this village. You could not ask for a safer, quieter place. But watching these shepherds in the gathering gloom, I'm struck by a sinister memory from my childhood: a vision of men walking in a row, with long sticks, equidistant across a grassy hill, like these fellows. I saw it on the television and it wasn't nice. They were policemen scouring desolate moors in northern England in 1965. They were looking for the bodies of children killed by Ian Brady and Myra Hindley, a pair of psychopaths who sometimes used a van to locate, abduct, and transport their victims. I was six years old. The TV reports scared the life out of me and instilled a nagging fear that would endure into my early teens.

I remember walking, trotting, then running home along suburban streets, after playing football in the park. I'd be worried sick, every time a car passed, in case it slowed down and someone jumped out to grab me. I'd arrive home, heart pounding, glad to be alive. I'd solemnly promise myself that tomorrow night, I'd come home earlier, before dark. But footy was too much fun. If you left early, you were a mummy's boy.

I can still feel it this evening, as an adult, looking out at the peaceful valleys: that gut-gnawing, skin-tingling dread of bad people in slow cars. *They'll spot me, sooner or later.*

Back in the house, browsing the Internet, I find no mention of organ snatchers in Culmea, nor in Romania. However, something must have sparked that story Dragoș heard in school. Perhaps they are out there, somewhere in the world, trundling around in their black vans. All roads lead to *The Daily Mail*, surprise, surprise.

According to that popular organ, the illegal international trade in kidneys, hearts, liver, and the rest is worth around $1 billion p.a. Surgeons in China, it seems, perform some 10,000 registered transplants a year, despite a scarcity of donors, and if you're wondering how come, the *Mail* has an answer. People are killed on demand: vagrants, political prisoners, members of Falun Gong, and so on. Their organs are *harvested*, like a crop, says the *Mail*. How sinister is that?

Next, from a less sensational source, I find a long-running story about Kosovo. It says that a report by a Swiss prosecutor to the Council of Europe found *credible, convergent indications* of organ theft from Serb prisoners of war, perpetrated by baddies linked to the Kosovo Liberation Army. On the other hand, war crimes investigators from the UN say there is insufficient evidence. So, perhaps we'll never know.

Next, I read about a twelve-year-old African boy smuggled into Britain by organ traders but saved from the butcher's block when immigration officials alerted the police. Lucky him.

The only reference to vans comes in a tragic tale from Turkey; a blogger recalls seeing vehicles plastered with hundreds of photos of missing kids thought to have been abducted by the local organ mafia, so-called. What a world.

I close the lid of my laptop and listen to cowbells clinking. We were probably right to tell little Dragoş not to worry about a black van. Then again, our remote mountain village would be an easy place for baddies to abduct a kid on a quiet lane. We should warn him, just in case, to be wary of strangers offering lifts. Standard advice to any kid, anywhere, I suppose. Better safe than sorry.

Angela stirs a big pot of rice pudding. "I must call Dragoș's mum and thank her for this milk."

"Be sure to tell her about the black van, Angela."

"Are you serious?"

"Yes, tell her what Dragoș said."

"Because?"

"First, she may not know how worried he is. Second, he should never accept lifts from strangers."

"I'm sure she tells him that. And I doubt there's a black van."

"Just a black cloud over his little head. I know the feeling."

"How do you mean, Mike?"

"Ever heard of The Moors Murderers?"

My wife looks puzzled. She puts down her wooden spoon and folds her arms. "I'm not sure I want to, but go on."

I tell her all about them. When I'm done, Angela looks as troubled I was, fifty-odd years ago. Just like Dragoș did today. He's probably huddled in bed right now, staring into darkness and listening for the distant drone of an engine. *They're coming.*

Ironic really, seeing as 'Dracula's Castle' is only three kilometres away from our village. Does little Dragoș know that's a load of old cobblers? Probably. Then again, perhaps he hangs garlic around his bed. I must ask, next time he brings the milk.

Man with a Plan

Dinu straddles the fence outside his house and offers helpful gestures as I park the car. *Left a bit.* Last time we met, he was wearing dog-chewed rubber clogs and rough socks. Today he's wearing proper shoes – presumably because we're going into town – plus a dark green leather jerkin, dark green pants, and a pointy hat made of dark brown felt. It matches his short, pointy beard. He's forty-plus but looks a lot younger, somehow, sitting there grinning like a sprite after a night of mischief.

I get out of the car and we shake hands. Dinu jerks a thumb towards a stack of logs all dark and wet from overnight rain.

"Lisa is hiding behind the woodpile. She knows something's up."

"Did you tell her she's going to the vet?"

"No, but even so, she's afraid. You should be careful when you put her in your car, she might bite."

"That's why you're going to help me, remember?"

"Fair enough, thanks for coming."

"A deal is a deal. This way, no more unwanted pups."

Dinu nods, tight-lipped. Least said, soonest mended.

I open the car's rear hatch. He whistles and a medium-sized, skinny brown dog trots from behind the logs, her ears down and tail wagging. Scared, yes. Aggressive, no. We lift Lisa gently into the car, cooing encouragement. She stands rigidly in the back, wide-eyed and panting. So far, so good. Dinu's elderly mother Doamna Aneta emerges from their little cottage, dressed all in black. She wriggles bony fingers through the car window, trying to caress the dog. "Poor little Lisa! See you soon, my petal."

Dinu settles into the passenger seat, clutching a scuffed leather satchel.

"Bye, Mama. I'll call you from the vet."

Driving away, I glance in my rear-view mirror. Aneta is waving her arms. She looks like a scarecrow in a windy field. Whatever, I'm glad she agreed. Glad she cares so much about her dog. Two months ago, she was dumping Lisa's puppies in the forest, in a sack. But we don't talk about that any more. Forward.

We bump around hairpin bends, down the forest road. Puddles twinkle in black mud. I drive slowly so as not to upset the dog, who seems upset enough. "Did Lisa eat last night, Dinu?"

"You told me not to feed her. She'll have an anaesthetic."

"Just checking, well done."

A middle-aged man and woman trudge uphill towards us, carrying several bags of shopping. She's wearing all black, including the headscarf. He wears a woollen waistcoat and an astrakhan hat. I know their faces, but not their names. As the car trundles past, they nod at us. They're grim-eyed and completely knackered, halfway through a seven-kilometre hike home.

Dinu sighs, shaking his head. "It's not right, the lack of public transport, especially for people like that with no car."

"No horse and cart either, by the look of it."

"They have one, I know them. But their son is probably out collecting *gunoi*. What's *gunoi* in English?"

"Dung. As in, cow dung, horse dung, and so on."

"Ah, yes, of course." Dinu turns for another look at the elderly couple. Or perhaps he's checking for dog dung in the back of my car.

"How's Lisa?" I ask.

"Scared."

We chat about public transport, or rather, the total absence of it around here. I tell Dinu about our neighbours – two teenage daughters who must trek up and down this mountain road, in all kinds of weather, just to get to school. He tells me about adults who leave home at 3 a.m., walk an hour, then ride for another hour on a bus, to work in a factory that makes dashboards for posh cars.

"It's not right, Domnul Mike."

"Agreed, Domnul Dinu. There should be a mini bus, at least. Actually, my wife and I wrote to the Mayor about that, among other things, six months ago."

"What did he say?"

"We're still waiting for a reply."

"Culmea seems medieval, sometimes. We live in the Dark Ages."

"But with excellent Internet, Dinu." I glance sideways into the dark forest. Romania also has one third of Europe's bears, and some of them live in there. I've seen their tracks in summer, big ones. It's a wonder people don't get attacked. *Walking this dirt road at 3 a.m.?* I'd be terrified.

We watch silver rainwater dribble down muddy gullies; it carves them deeper by the day.

"What about asphalt, Dinu, would you put some on our roads, if you were mayor?"

"Bad idea, it would bring too many fast jeeps full of rich tourists."

"Whose money would help the local economy."

"Agreed, but have you tried driving a horse and cart up a steep asphalt road, in bad weather? The hooves slide. No, thank you."

It's a fair point, and one I've heard before. But what catches my ear is Dinu's impressive command of English. *Hooves? Slide?* There's something else, too: he sounds almost British, with traces of Cockney at times. How come? Why no American accent, like so many Romanians who learned English from Hollywood movies? Maybe he grew up watching *The Sweeney*, instead.

"Domnul Mike?"

"Yes, Domnul Dinu?"

"Something we must discuss. When you have time."

"How about now?"

"Later, I want to show you a book."

"Which book?"

"An important one, you'll see."

Perhaps he means religion. I hear Dinu and his Mama are Born Again Christians. He does look a bit like Jesus: dark-eyed, wispy beard, mission impossible. It all fits, except the accent.

Dinu points at a huge pothole. "Mind the gap."

He sounds like the announcer on the Tube. *Ah, perhaps he lived in London?* I drive in zig zags, avoiding cavities, craters, and anything else that might wreck the bank account. Dinu claps his hands, three times, gently. "Well done, that man!"

Now he's a cricket commentator and I'm intrigued.

"Where did you learn English, Dinu?"

"Long story."

"We've got fifteen minutes to go, is that enough?"

"Well, yes, I suppose. Put it this way, I knew, from an early age, that Romania was a strange place. I wanted to live in a different country. But I needed English, the international language. So, when I was fourteen years old, I devised a plan in three parts, all connected."

"Why three?"

Dinu leans forward in his seat, rubbing his palms together, warming to the theme. He tells me about part one: he worked hard on English at school. Very hard. So hard, his teacher would cite his achievements for his classmates to emulate.

"She'd point at me, and say, 'If Dinu can do it, why can't you?' *Pour encourager les autres*, you see."

"You speak French as well?"

"Yes. That's another reason she called me her *prize pupil*."

Dinu points at a pothole, and I swerve. Claws scrape behind us and Lisa whines. Dinu comforts her. *There-there.*

"And the second part of your plan?" I ask.

"Leave school, join the merchant navy. Part three was to jump ship in an Anglophone port. But everything changed in 1989, with the revolution, so-called."

"When Ceaușescu jumped in a helicopter."

"Exactly. I had just left school. That was that."

We sit in silence. I'm thinking about Romania's batty, brutal, collectivist regime. It ruined a lot of places but not these remote mountains where subsistence farming will probably last forever, unless the mayor lays asphalt *pour encourager les touristes.*

"After '89," says Dinu, "we could go wherever we wanted, sort of. I didn't need a big plan anymore, just a destination."

"So, you upped and left?"

"For London, yes. To stay with a friend. I painted three doors for his landlord. Next thing, I'm getting jobs all over London. Well paid, too. I even turned some down, to have a little free time. All work and no play makes John a dull boy."

"Not to mention Jack. How did you spend your free time?"

"In the British Library. I suppose you have been there?"

I shake my head in mute shame. Dinu stares and pushes back his conical felt hat. He cannot believe his elfin ears. "Why not, Mike, if you lived in Britain?"

"Good question. Anyway, what did you read?"

"DIY books, mostly."

I ease the car around a muddy bend and spot a man wobbling along ahead of us in a world of his own. He turns and waves his arms. It's Viorel from our village. Drunk as several skunks, by the look of it. He's wearing overalls and a battered cap, just about. I slow down, wondering what to do. Decency says offer Viorel a lift, but he can be quite a nuisance. He likes to hit animals, start arguments, and make salacious comments at passing women – including my wife. Frankly, I'd prefer to let the bugger walk. But let's be nice, give him a chance.

"Why are you beeping your horn?" says Dinu.

"To offer this guy a lift." I beckon Viorel towards the car. He grins at me, tongue out, and looks demented. Or perhaps I'm demented. Oh well, birds of a feather. He lurches towards us, taking the scenic route, pausing to stare at an impressive pothole.

"But surely you know who that is?" says Dinu.

"Who doesn't."

"And you'll pick him up?"

"If he wants a ride, yes. Love thy neighbour and so on."

"I'm glad he's not my neighbour."

"Me too. Let's hope he behaves himself. Here he comes."

Viorel clambers into the back seat and yaps non-stop in a loud voice, poking his finger in my shoulder. He's on his way to town to buy stamps and see some friends.

"For a tea. Just a tea. How is your wife, Domnul Mike?"

"She's fine, thank you."

Viorel clicks his teeth. "Very nice, your wife."

Dinu glances at me as if reading my troubled mind.

Viorel points. "It was here that I saw the wolves."

Dinu smiles, bemused. "You mean dogs, Viorel?"

Viorel nods, vigorously. "Wolves, aye, four of 'em. At midnight. Came out of the forest and stopped just there. I lit my cigarette lighter and waved it, to scare them. They ran off. Four wolves. Almost shit my pants, honest to God."

Dinu chuckles. Perhaps he's heard it before. "You're lucky to be alive, Viorel."

"I know it, mate."

"We need public transport."

"Good idea, but it will never happen."

"Because?" I ask.

Viorel pokes my shoulder. I look in the mirror. He's rubbing his thumb and finger together. *Money.*

The dirt road snakes down into a wide valley – the remnants of a former limestone quarry – where rocks the size of dustbins can tumble down when you least expect. I glance left and right, just in case. Viorel pokes my shoulder and says, "Don't worry, Domnul, no wolves in daylight."

We stop in town, near the post office. He tumbles out of the car, walks around it, then reappears at my window to tap with a gnarled knuckle. "Do you know there's a dog in the back?"

"Yes, Viorel, we're taking it to the vet."

"Good idea. Now another question. Can you lend me ten lei to buy stamps? It's for stamps, you see."

"No, Viorel, sorry."

"Good day, Domnul Mike." He walks away, then back again. "And thank you for the ride, I must say."

"My pleasure, Viorel."

He wobbles past the Post Office and vanishes through an open door with a sign above it: *Carlsberg.* Presumably, they sell stamps, too.

We reach the veterinary surgery in good time. Dinu coaxes a terrified Lisa from the back of the car and she slithers between us, her tail curled tight beneath her tummy.

Cosmin the vet comes out to meet us wearing his usual uniform of smart green smock, blue jeans, and snazzy New Balance trainers. He's tall, slim, and good-looking in a boyish way, although his greying hair and stubble lend him an air of authority. He crouches down to greet Lisa, then shepherds Dinu and me towards a picnic table with benches, in his rose garden.

"Can you wait out here, please? It's a bit busy inside today, sorry, but this won't take long. Back soon."

He leads the dog towards the lobby. Three teenage girls sit inside, on wooden chairs. The middle girl clutches a sleepy cat wrapped in a towel and looks sad. The others watch Cosmin breeze past and exchange wistful smiles. *He's cute.* Dinu and I retire to the picnic benches. The roses are blooming lovely, all pink and perfumed. Spring has sprung, although a silver mist shrouds distant mountains. We should've brought a picnic. *Ah, I know.* I open my rucksack, extract a wooden chess box, and place it on the table.

"My wife and I usually bring this. Care for a game, Dinu?"

"No thanks, I want to discuss something more important, except it's in my satchel, in the car. Can you give me the keys?"

I hand them over and Dinu strides away. I wander the lawn, admiring roses in a neat border. They're better than the ones in our yard. *How come?* It's an intriguing puzzle, but I wonder why I'm wondering. Not so long ago, I couldn't have cared less about gardens. I must be growing old.

Cosmin reappears. "All set! Dog is sedated and shaved." He points at the chess box. "Nice, very. Are you playing chess?"

"No, we're going to discuss something more important."

"Like what?"

"The Bible, I reckon."

"I didn't know you were religious."

53

"I'm not, but Domnul Dinu is. Born again, it seems."

"Good for him. Once is enough for me." Cosmin inspects my chess set. "Mother of pearl. Where from?"

"Egypt."

"Wow, you went to Egypt?"

"No, Angela did. This little piggy stayed home."

"I want to go to Egypt. You want to hear a joke?"

"If it's funny."

"OK, so, there are two cops, and one says, *What's chess?* And the other cop says, *It's the bits we put away before we play backgammon.* Funny, eh? Thought you'd like it. Anyway, back soon. Tell your friend Dan, *no worries.* His dog is healthy, which makes a change, coming from your village. Dinu, I mean. Just saying."

Cosmin scoots away in his funky shoes and the teenage girls smile as he flits by. Even the sad one with the sleepy cat, this time.

Dinu returns clutching his satchel. It probably contains The Good News and he's going to share it, any minute now, lucky me. I fold my arms, wondering how to say, *pagan, actually,* in Romanian. *Păgân, de fapt?* That should do it.

He squats astride the bench, reaches into his satchel, and extracts a heavy, hardback book. The cover has a colour photo of spectacular mountains under an unlikely blue sky, with a cute little train in a gorge. A man in a red sweater, booted and backpacked, stands with a woman in a yellow hat. He's pointing. *Can you see the spectacular mountains?* Either he's dim or she's shortsighted. It's the sort of book you might find on a coffee table, but not ours. The title is in German. What's *The Bible* in German? No idea. I gaze in vain for a telltale cross on the mountains, like in Romania.

"Nice book, Dinu, what's it about?"

He points at the cover. "Look at this little train."

"The train?"

"It's just what we need. A train to run up and down from our village to the town. We can buy one, second-hand, from Austria. I know a woman who sells them. We just need the money. I'm thinking we should team up. You and me. What d'you say?"

I stare at the book. It's one thing to help Dinu get his dog shaved and zapped, but buying a railway from Heidi? No thanks. My wife would boot me down the mountain.

"Dinu, what are you talking about?"

"Public transport, of course." Dinu flicks more pages. "See? Little trains in the mountains. It's the solution to our problem in Culmea. Have you been to Austria?"

"Yes."

"Me too. Did you see all the little trains?"

"No, just mountains. And cows. And shops selling Mozart chocolate. How do you mean, *team up?*"

"I've got lots of land. I've identified a slope with a suitable gradient. All we need is track and rolling stock. We could convert it to renewable power, perhaps. What do you think? We just need the money. We could all apply to the European Union. We just need a plan. The first part is the land, and I've got that."

Dinu is breathless. I'm speechless. On the one hand, applying to the European Union certainly sounds better than applying to me, but on the other, big questions remain.

"Dinu, who's *all?* You said, *we could all apply?*"

"Me, you, and the people in our village. We could start an NGO, non-profit. Or even a company, for profit."

Dinu has a twinkle in his eye, and possibly a bat in his belfry. I sit back to keep it out of mine. *The people in our village?* They can't even agree to install water meters that cost ten euros, never mind set up a mountain railway that would cost half a bloody million. I don't want to rain on Dinu's platform, but this is the last thing I expected. He flicks glossy pages, pointing here and there. *Train. In the mountains. Another train. In the mountains.* But the book smells musty and his idea smells fishy. *Is he kidding? European funds?* Imagine the bureaucracy, the time, and the paperwork. I'd be out my depth. My wife and I have already written to the Mayor about transport. Fat lot of good it did, too. Now this? So much for a friendly lecture on Jesus.

"What's wrong, Domnul Mike? Are you upset? You think I'm crazy, I suppose? Oh, well, that's ok, so does Mama. My sister too, for that matter. But I'm not crazy if that's what you think. Is that what you think, Domnul Mike?"

"No, actually, I think you're very ambitious. Good for you. I mean, good luck with your plan. But this is not what I was expecting, I suppose."

"Were you expecting to play chess? Sorry, I don't play chess. Books are what I like. Books are very helpful. You look surprised. Well, so am I. Don't you like reading?"

"Of course. It's just, I thought you wanted to discuss God."

Dinu closes his book and stares at the roses. He seems disappointed but not for long.

"Very well, let's discuss God. What did you want to know?"

How to cure Chickenpox

The sky is too bright and the breeze is too cold, out here in our yard. The locals would say today's weather is sunny with teeth – *e soare cu dinți*. In other words, I need a warm coat.

Besides, my watch says 10.45, and the fumes from my pot of creosote are giving me a fuzzy head, which means I've earned a break. I've daubed twenty fence posts so far. *Thirty more to do?* They can wait. I wrap my paintbrush in a rag, put the lid on the pot and walk up the sloping garden towards the house.

Our dogs are barking through the fence at a man in the lane. He's wearing baggy pants and worn-out wellies. I recognise the pork pie hat and wobbly gait. He lurches about like a puppet on strings. He gestures and mutters, as if rehearsing lines for an argument recently lost. He waves at me and almost stumbles.

"Domnul Mike, *ce faci?*" He has piggy eyes and a foxy grin.

"Fine thanks, Domnul Vasile, and you?"

He points. "Your dogs."

"Yeah, sorry about the noise."

"They don't like me when I'm…" Vasile pauses to admire the mountains, then sighs and continues on his wayward, well-oiled, but at least he didn't pee in our lane. The locals say Vasile is blotting paper – *sugativă*. They have a way with words and certainly don't mince 'em. I wonder, sometimes, what they say about Angela and me.

Entering the house, I tease off my boots then greet the four young kids who are huddled around our big table and scribbling in their exercise books. Angela is writing on her whiteboard:

Every cloud has a silver lining.

She turns from her task. "How's it going out there, Mike?"

"*E soare cu dinți.*" I wink at the kids and little Grigore winks back.

"Can you suggest any English proverbs for us?" says Angela,

"A stitch in time saves nine."

"That's a good one. Got any more?"

I fill a glass at the tap. "You don't miss your water until your well runs dry."

"Great, thanks. Another one?"

"The early bird catches the worm in a bottle of tequila."

"Sorry?"

"Just kidding. Guess who the dogs were barking at?"

"Vasile. I saw him through the window. He started early today."

"Perhaps he's finishing late."

"Did he pee against the fence?"

"No, oddly enough."

"Glad to hear it. Oh well, back to work." Angela writes my suggestions on the white board. She's got

English on the left and Romanian on the right. But they don't match, even I can see that.

"What's that list on the right, Angela?"

"Local folklore. For example, the top line says that if you pick a *garofița* flower, then lightning will strike your house."

"*Garofița*. The tiny, violet one?"

"Yes, but you don't see them often, so perhaps this saying is just a clever way to protect a rare plant."

"Interesting. What's your second line, about a house fire?"

"If you destroy a stork's nest, the stork will burn your house."

"How?"

Angela turns to her students and asks for a volunteer to explain. Dark-eyed Maria in the green bonnet rises to her feet and tells me that a stork will drop hot embers on my roof. She's dead serious, all frowns. *You're dead.* I drain my glass of water. *Cheers.*

"Bye, everyone, and good luck. Oh, where's Emil today?"

"Sick with *varicelă*," says Angela, "chickenpox."

"Poor Emil."

"He'll miss your ukulele class, too, and a school trip to the bear sanctuary. Then again, it all depends."

"On the doctor?"

"On what colour clothes Emil wears," Angela says, with a chuckle.

"Come again?"

Angela turns to her class. "The cure for chickenpox, Maria?"

For a second time, Maria rises to the occasion. "Emil must wear lots of red clothes. As many as possible. To get better."

"Why red clothes?"
"Because they bring out the rash, Domnul Mike."
"Did a doctor tell you that?"
"No, but it's true, ask anyone."

Walking back to my tub of creosote, I crouch to inspect some bright green leaves growing wild. I tug one off, crush it in my palm, and inhale the aroma. It smells like toothpaste and helps clear my head. I look towards the mountains. Strange to think our planet was rock and slime, once upon a time. But now look, it's lush and buzzing. *Amazing place, planet Earth.* Then I remember something else that Romanians say: *Nu freca menta*. Stop rubbing the mint. That's when you're wasting time, like now.

Walking the dogs, Angela and I stop outside Emil's house to chat with his grandmother Doamna Regina, a short, stout widow with a wrinkled brow and no-nonsense manner. She's waving a stick at some noisy sheep. They're bleating bonkers, quite aggressive and poking slimy grey tongues at us. *Nee-eh.* It's all a bit weird. Some of them trot closer to investigate us, much to the delight of our gasping dogs. We pull back, lest they lunge for the kill. The sheep, that is.

Angela compliments Doamna Regina on her new hairstyle. Regina caresses her perm. "For Easter, *mulțumesc.*" She wags her stick at the sheep. "Go back, you lot!" They scamper away.

"Why are they so noisy?" I ask.

"Looking for their lambs, Domnul Mike."

I glance around. "Are the lambs in a different field?"

"They're dead." Doamna Regina draws a fingernail across her neck. "We killed twenty-four to sell in the market for Easter." She looks almost apologetic. "But that's life around here."

Perhaps she's remembered I'm a vegetarian from far away.

"How's Emil's chickenpox?" says Angela. "Pity he missed the school trip to the bear sanctuary."

"Actually, he enjoyed it. They've got some big ones."

"Oh, the other kids told me Emil was too sick and couldn't go."

"He was, last week."

"Doesn't it take two or three weeks to recover from chickenpox?"

"I made him wear lots of red."

"To cure it?" I suggest.

Doamna Regina nods. "And I put nine beans on his tummy."

"Beans on his tummy?"

"Yes, like this, in a row." Doamna Regina carefully places nine invisible beans, mid-air, with a finger and thumb. She glances around and says quietly, "Old wives' remedies but they work."

"Certainly seems so," says Angela, raising an eyebrow at me.

"Do you know a local cure for alcoholism, Doamna Regina?"

"Yes, Domnul Mike, stop drinking."

"I didn't mean me. Well, not yet anyway."

Regina tilts her permed head. "So, who did you mean?"

But that would be telling and, as the Talmud says, *gossip kills three.*

Love Thy Neighbour

Our trusty little jeep jiggles up the steep forest road, growling like a dog at each hairpin bend. From the passenger seat, I'm scanning dense woodland on the left and right, hoping to glimpse wild deer. Local kids saw a bear last week, or so I heard.

Something big and brown emerges from the dense foliage a hundred metres ahead of us and steps into the road. My eyes pop, but it's just a bandy-legged fellow who has probably been for a pee in the bushes. He's wearing a baggy suit. I know that hat, too.

"There's what's-his-name, the friendly old fellow with a stammer."

"Let's offer him a ride. I'll slow down and you ask," says Angela.

"Will do. Is he Gheorghe or Ion?"

"Trifa, but it's a silly nickname. Just call him *Domnul*."

I lower my window as we approach. *"Bună ziua Domnul, veniți cu noi?"*

Trifa grins and raises his little brown hat. He has carp lips, a drinker's nose, and an engaging grin. He clambers aboard clutching a frayed canvas shopping bag, and slumps onto the back seat, placing his hat in his lap.

"*M-m-mulțumesc*, you are m-m-most kind."

He sounds exhausted and I'm not surprised. It's a long steep hike to Culmea and he's what, seventy-ten?

"Been to Dumbrăvița, Domnul?" says Angela.

"No, to Brașov c-c-courthouse."

"Oh, legal problems?"

"I'll say." Trifa dabs his brow with a handkerchief. "A very c-c-complicated case. Those lawyers are getting rich."

"How long has it taken, so far?" I ask.

"Two years."

"And what's the problem?

Trifa explains, in laborious detail, how a woman bought the guest house on the hill opposite his cottage. They became friendly neighbours until she banned him from driving his horse and cart on a dirt road across her fields. It was his short-cut, but no longer.

"Which means, for the last two years, I've had to use a narrow path that goes around and around. I must carry everything by hand or in saddlebags on my horse. This means an extra five hundred m-m-metres. Can you imagine the inconvenience, especially in bad weather? And what if my home c-c-catches fire? How will the fire engine s-s-save me? She's a witch, that Elvira. So, I took her to c-c-court. But I'm still waiting. It's all too much."

"Elvira with the blonde hair?" says Angela.

"Blonde my foot," Trifa snorts, "she uses peroxide. I saw the empty bottle in her bin outside *Casa Alpina*. That's what she calls the guest house now: *Casa Alpina*. Who does she think she is? Our mountains are not Alps, we're in the Carpathians, as any f-f-fool knows."

"We do have an alpine climate, though," I say. "Apparently, that's what stops our fruit trees from growing. Well, sometimes."

Trifa gives me a pained look. *WTF?* Perhaps I should be quiet.

"Why did Elvira ban you from using the short cut?" says Angela.

Trifa leans forward. His beak pokes between us. "Because that's how she is, she's a f-f-foreigner." He gazes at the forest. Justice is out there, somewhere.

"Actually, she's from Bucharest," Angela suggests.

"As I said, a *foreigner*."

"And how did it go, today, in the courthouse?" I ask.

"Waste of time, Domnul Mike, more delays."

"So, what happens now?"

"I'm going home to have some soup."

We reach the last hairpin bend, the road levels off, and our passenger climbs out, wheezing gratitude. "I'll bring you some eggs, one of these days."

He steps over a stile onto a narrow footpath and ambles bow-legged towards lilac trees whose pale purple buds droop in bunches like tiny grapes.

Sunshine glitters on the shiny windows of *Casa Alpina*, but Trifa's little pink cottage nearby looks old and somewhat sunken, just like its owner.

"I feel sorry for him," says Angela, as we drive on.

Sure as eggs, Trifa brings us twelve big ones a few days later, plus a kilo of white *urdă*, the local ricotta cheese. He grins, thrusting a plastic bag at Angela.

"Thank you, Doamna, for the l-l-lift. Most k-kind."

We invite him in for tea but he declines the offer and strides down the lane, planting his stick at regular intervals. We watch him go. "He's decent," I say.

"So is this *urdă*," says Angela, peeping into the bag. "Smells nice and fresh. I'll make some cheesecake."

By late afternoon, our dogs are pawing at the back door and cocking their heads at every window, prancing and whining. *Time for you-know-walkies.*

"Looks like rain," I say, eyeing the sky. *So much for spring.* We zip ourselves into our waxy waterproof coats, pull on our winter hats, and off we go.

The gasping hounds drag us forwards, pausing only to sniff a fence post or gobble sheep poo. *Mmm, delicious.*

A man appears on the lane, walking towards us. He's sheltering under an umbrella with a floral motif – huge daisies, pink and yellow. He moves slowly, sidestepping puddles.

"Isn't that Călin?" I say.

Angela glances up. "Looks like."

Călin's lurid umbrella billows in the wind, trying to flip inside out. He spins in circles, wrestling it back into shape. His tweed jacket is too big and his old canvas rucksack is vintage 1950, but, as ever, he has a certain style. Shirt and tie, always. Probably the best-dressed shepherd for hills around. Handsome fellow too, square-jawed with a piercing gaze. He'd make a good James Bond. *James Bondescu,* maybe. Except for that bizarre brolly. He raises it in greeting as we approach.

"Hello, Domnul Mike. *Bună ziua,* Doamna Angela."

I shake his wet hand. "*Yah-soo,* Domnul Călin."

"Ah, well done, so you remembered how to speak Greek?"

"I've been practising."

"Didn't I teach you *goodbye,* too?"

"I'm saving that for later. How are things?"

"Been fixing a roof for my mother-in-law. You?"

"Enjoying this lovely sunshine, thanks."

"Hah!"

We walk three abreast, with the dogs in front. Călin wants our opinions on Brexit, on the street protests around Romania, and on Domnul Trump. It makes a pleasant change since most young men around here usually want to talk about Spanish footballers they adore or German cars they cannot afford. I reckon Călin's years working in Athens have expanded his horizons. Why did he move back to Romania? *I must ask, sometime.* Perhaps his wife missed her family. She's local, as far I recall.

"And Trump?" says Călin.

"Romania should build a wall to keep him out."

"Is this British humour, Domnul Mike?"

"British weather, certainly. Where's spring?"

"Still asleep. I'm getting wet."

"Even with your nice umbrella."

"It's not mine, I borrowed it from my mother-in-law."

We reach a sharp bend and Călin's customary short-cut through a gap in the blackthorn bushes. I'm trying to remember *goodbye* in Greek, but he continues along the lane with us. Perhaps he's enjoying our chat, despite the rain. Perhaps he has business, up ahead.

We trudge and talk for another three hundred metres and arrive at a muddy T-junction. Călin bids us farewell. "Nice to see you, now I'm going home."

"Oh, why didn't you take the short-cut, back there?" I ask.

"Not allowed, these days. Strongly forbidden, in fact."

"By whom?"

"My neighbour. I was threatened with an axe."

"Because you used that short-cut?" says Angela.

"Yes, across land which is not mine."

"Hmm, this is new. What changed?"

Călin chuckles. "People change. That's how they are, around here. In Romanian, we say this: *N-ai să vezi țigan harnic și brănean darnic.*"

"You'll never see a hard-working gypsy or generous Brănean," says Angela, presumably for my benefit, and just as well.

"Exactly," says Călin, "even my wife agrees and she's from Bran. Have you heard this expression, Mike?"

"Not until today, although, to be fair, we know plenty of hard-working gypsies. Talented, too."

Călin shrugs. "But have you met a nice Brănean?"

"Well, I think we've made a few friends here."

"You *think* so, Doamna Angela."

"Well, you're our friend, Călin."

"I'm from Oltenia, in south-west Romania, don't forget. Here is very different. Here, you take a short-cut, you watch out."

"Sounds familiar. Do you know Domnul Trifa?"

Călin laughs aloud. "Trifa? Of course, why?"

"Because he's in a similar situation."

"Really, he told you so?"

"Yes, it seems Doamna Elvira will not allow Trifa to drive his cart along her path, near *Casa Alpina*."

"Actually, that's my neighbour."

"Doamna Elvira threatened you with an axe?" says Angela.

"No, Trifa did. My short-cut was across his land, you see."

Angela looks at me. "Must be a different Trifa."

I look at Călin. "Trifa who wears a brown hat?"

Călin nods. "With a feather, if he finds a nice one. There is only one Trifa in Culmea. I should know."

"Do you know about his court case against Elvira?"

"Everyone knows. I even mentioned it when Trifa told me not to walk on his land because it seemed to me, how do you say in English: *ironic*."

"And what did Trifa say?"

"That's when he fetched his axe."

I'm lost for words. Angela just shakes her head. The sky rumbles and flickers. The rain fills potholes until they can take no more and the water spills over.

"Do you ever read the Bible, Domnul Mike?"

"Not since I was a school kid, Domnul Călin, why?"

"In the Bible, a kind-hearted king takes pity on a merchant who is in prison for a debt to the royal family. The king releases the merchant and erases his debt. The merchant goes home, summons a poor farmer who owes him money, beats him and throws him in prison."

"I do like a happy ending."

"I haven't finished yet. The king finds out and says to that bad merchant, *How dare you? Why not follow my example and forgive that poor farmer?* Then, the king puts the merchant back in prison and throws away the key. It's in the Bible. True story. What do you think about it?"

Angela pokes her walking stick into a puddle. The brown rainwater swirls like milky coffee.

"I think that what goes around, comes around, Călin."

"Yes, sometimes it does, Doamna, but not always."

"Have you told that story to Trifa?"

"No, Domnul Mike, but perhaps I will. *La revedere.*"

"*La revedere,*" says Angela, "and be careful."

Călin raises the umbrella above his head. "Bye!"

The Greek comes back to me, just in time. *"Antio."*

"You remembered," says Călin, walking away.

The dogs drag us in the opposite direction, tracking a scent along the squelchy lane. Far below, in a wide valley, the ancient town of Bran huddles in deep mist. What a sight. It could be a photo in a guidebook.

"We should walk down there, sometime," says Angela.

"When the weather improves."

"Summer is coming, Mike. We'll take a picnic."

"Dogs would love a long hike. Three hours, round trip?"

"Perhaps there's a short-cut."

"You first."

Palincashire

The beefy young farmer ambles up the dirt road outside our yard, whistling a merry tune. He pauses to grin at me through the garden fence. His round face is bright red from lots of sun. If a tomato could smile, it would look like Horia.

"Cutting your grass, eh, Domnul Mike?"

"Yes, Horia, but not very well."

"Want me to sharpen your scythe, good and proper?"

"One of these days, yes please. Blade needs a good beating."

Horia points across the yard. "Can I borrow your hosepipe, seeing as you're not using it?"

I lay down my scythe and wipe my brow. "Sure, today?"

"If possible. Just thought I'd ask, since I'm passing. I'll pick it up on my way back and carry it home, how's that?"

"I have a better idea. That hosepipe is heavy and your place is quite a walk, so I'll drive you. I need a break, to be honest."

"Right you are, Domnul Mike, see you in fifteen minutes."

He grins again. Funny how things turn out, once foes become friends. Eighteen months ago, Horia was rolling up his sleeves, ready for a scrap. With me. And now look – bezzie mates.

"Oh, shall I come in and do your blade, Domnul Mike?"

"No thanks, Horia. My dogs haven't forgotten."

I gesture across the yard, where Linda and Sam glare at him with their ears pricked. They lope closer, prowling and growling. Any minute now, they'll be barking mad. Because this fellow beat them with a stick, two summers ago. They deserved it, mind you, for killing one of his sheep. Tunnelled under this fence and tore the poor thing to bits, they did. Horia found them with it in the lane and gave them a thrashing. I was next, almost.

"Hi, Linda." He clicks his teeth.

Linda trots to the fence and shows him hers.

My old Suzuki jeep bumpity bumps along the pot-holed dirt road to Horia's place. Did someone say *road*? I feel as if I'm driving across Mars. Some of these ruts run half a metre deep, gouged every spring by our fast-flowing snowmelt then baked to an unyielding concretion by the summer sun. If I had the money I'd buy a Humvee. *Buy two, in fact, for when the first one breaks.*

Horia sways alongside me, chuckling. His sausage fingers grip the dashboard; his sheep stare from a meadow as we pass, and his cows flick their tails. We're listening to Muddy Waters: *I'm going down to Louisiana, behind the sun.* Actually, we're just going down to the last house. Horia lives at the end of the known world and probably prefers it that way. He whistles along to the song, and seems happy enough, despite the bone-jarring terrain.

"You like blues music, eh?" I ask.

"Is this blues, Domnul Mike?"

"Delta blues."

"My friend went to the delta on holiday. Caught lots of fish."

"You mean the Danube delta, right?"

"Left, and mind my gate."

I park in Horia's tidy little yard. He hauls my heavy hosepipe onto his broad shoulders, saunters to a standpipe, and hooks it up. The view from his land is stupendous – mountains rise steeply from lush valleys and a breeze ripples across deep grass, making it seem to run uphill in the haze. It's a lovely day. I'd better get back to my scything. Make a mess while the sun shines, and so on.

"I'll be off then, Horia."

"Right you are, Domnul Mike, but first come and see my calf, she's a beauty." He leads me to a little shed. "Mind your head."

It's dark and warm inside, with a nice smell. There's a horse, two fluffy lambs, hens on a perch, and a beautiful calf curled in a swathe of hay on the floor. It glances up at us with big glassy eyes that could turn you into a vegetarian at fifty paces. All we need is an ox, an ass, and Baby Jesus in a manger. "Like it?" says Horia.

"Lovely."

That cute calf will soon be veal, perhaps, but that's life, up here, at least for some. Short and sweet. Poor little bugger.

"Come and see my pig. He's a beauty, too."

"Don't mind if I do."

We leave the barn and walk across the yard, watched by a huge, scabby-arsed cat with a manky eye. Horia doesn't mention him.

We reach a brick hut and Horia says, "Mind your head."

I mind my head but he forgot my nose. The place reeks. A large, hairy porker peers out at us from a cage of rusty iron bars. This not-so-little piggy looks bored shitless, which explains the smell.

"You like him, Domnul Mike?"

"Yes, Horia. Does he ever get out?"

"Out where?"

"In the fresh air. For a wander in your field. He'd be a lot happier."

"Happier?"

"Pigs are very intelligent."

Horia looks at the pig and then at me as if trying to decide who's smarter. "He'll dig up my field, this pig."

"But moles do that already, so what's the difference?"

"I can't sell moles at Christmas."

He's got me there. But his prisoner is urging me on. I can see it in those piggy eyes. "Happy animals make tastier meat, Horia, which would mean more cash for you."

"How do you work that out, Domnul Mike?"

"Happiness produces hormones. Organic farming. It's a fact."

"Organic? You can't get more *bio-bio* than my farm."

"Well, yes, I agree. Your hens, cows, and sheep get a good deal. But not this pig. You should let him out. I would."

"Do you have pigs?"

"No, but…well, never mind. I should be getting back."

"One last thing. Come next door. Mind your head."

It's helpful advice, seeing as all these doorways seem designed for midgets, which is odd since Horia is not a midget. Perhaps by law, when you build a farm up here, you must ensure that people can easily bash their brains out. But laws have changed, now we're in the EU. My head dips and a question arises.

"Your doorways are a bit low, Horia, how come?"

"You're a bit tall. Follow me."

We cross the yard and descend a short flight of brick steps. Horia nudges at another tiny door. There should be a blue plaque: *Tom Thumbescu Lived Here.* In we go, stooping low, easy does it.

We enter a cramped cellar stashed with little wooden barrels, huge plastic tubs, sagging sacks of grain, dusty bottles, petrified paint brushes that belong in a bin, and scary-looking, rusty implements not used since the Transylvanian Inquisition.

Horia prises the lid off a plastic tub and invites me to peep inside at a load of rotten apples floating in gooey liquid. The sharp aroma makes my eyes water. I think I've had enough organic farming. I'd like to go home please, but Horia has other ideas, thank you.

"In a few months, I'll transfer this to my copper still."

"Ah, right, Horia. To make *palinca*?"

"Exactly. Do you like *palinca*?"

"Good *palinca*, yes, I do. Is yours any good?"

Horia smiles. *Stupid question.* I smile back. Bezzie mates. Funny how things turn out. He produces a bottle and two tiny glasses. Perhaps he wants to get me pie-eyed and put me in a pie.

"Fancy just a little one, Domnul Mike?"

I muse for a moment about the short drive home across Mars. I should probably say *no.*

"Yes please."

Horia pours *palinca*, clear as spring water, and raises his glass.

"To friends and neighbours."

"Friends and neighbours."

I take a little sip. The hooch trickles down with a fiery kick. It tastes of apples and smells like an orchard in summer. "Wow, this is good."

"Twice distilled and forty percent, Domnul Mike."

We chat for a little while and Horia tells me that *palinca* can be made from all sorts – apples, pears, plums, you name it. Throw them in a barrel, let it all ferment, boil it up, then wait for the good stuff to drip-drip. It's not rocket science. Just rocket fuel, if you get it wrong. Horia got it right. Because he knows how, I can tell.

"You could do it too, Domnul Mike. You can use my still."

"To make *palinca?* I have a better idea. I'll just drink yours."

"Hah!"

We toast his calf. Then we toast his pig.

I drive slowly home, glad I departed after *just a little one.* Two glasses of that and I'd probably end up in a ditch, wheels spinning. I sing along to Muddy Waters, who is *Rollin' and Tumblin'*. He mentions his barrel house and I remember why. It was in his biography. He brewed moonshine.

When I get home, Angela is mixing fragrant goo in a plastic bowl. *Banana cake, lucky us.* She listens to my pitch then says, "You're not serious?"

"Actually, I am. I want to make hooch, like Muddy Waters. Except with Horia. He's got a copper still. You should see his apples, he's got loads fermenting, ready to go in it."

"Because he's got apple trees and years of experience. What will you brew?"

"Horia says you can make *palinca* out of any fruit. I'll ask him to teach me. But first, we need fruit. Old stuff will do. So, instead of throwing it on our compost heap, let's stick it in a tub to ferment. We'll have enough by autumn, when Horia brews his *palinca*. You don't need those, do you?" I point at three sloppy banana skins.

Angela turns to look. "You want to ferment them?"

"Got to start somewhere."

"Mike, Romanians don't make *palinca* from bananas."

"I'm not Romanian. Africans make banana beer, remember?"

"You're not African, remember?"

"Whatever, we'll make tropical *palinca*. Might taste good."

"We?"

Day by day, week by week, my tub fills with old fruit. Any that we don't eat goes straight in: squishy apples, dodgy oranges, crappy old kiwi, even the scaly skin of a pineapple. When Angela adds carrot peelings as if to make a point, I gaze into my tub with a pang of proprietorial angst.

"Carrots, Angela?"

"Why not? Might taste good."

By early autumn, we've got a fifty-litre plastic barrel full of fragrant, fruity mash, with a little yeast and sugar thrown in for hubble and bubble. So far, so good, but Horia's not an easy man to find even by phone. I try several times, over several days. Eventually, he answers but seems to have forgotten our chat about making *palinca*. He sounds surprised when I mention the contents of my tub.

"You put *what* in it, Domnul Mike?"
"Anything and everything."
"Who told you to do that?"

Horia's curiosity gets the better of his scepticism, however, and one day he turns up to inspect our barrel. I prise the lid off and Horia peeps in, rubbing his sunburnt nose. "Interesting smell."

"We've gone tropical."
His bemused expression says we've gone bananas.
"Certainly frothy, Domnul Mike, which means it's ready. What about tomorrow, around noon? Vlad and Bella Bănică will bring their barrel, too. Best to do it all at once, while my still is hot."
"I'll be there."
"Come early so you can tend the fire."
"No problem. What will you do?"
"Something else."

I drive across Mars' southern hemisphere to Horia's house and find him around the back, down the hill, crouching at two old oil drums that stand a metre apart. A narrow copper pipe runs horizontally between them at head height. I'm intrigued, already. So, this is where we'll make *palinca.* Or rather, where he will.

I haul Tub Tropicana from the back of my jeep. The tub weighs quite a bit, especially if you're a skinny wretch. I drag it backwards across rough grass. Horia is stuffing balls of newspaper and bits of scrap wood into a recess cut into the side of one of the drums, near the bottom. He glances up as I approach.

"Once I get this fire lit, you take over and keep it going, ок, Domnul Mike?"

"No problem, Horia. When are Vlad and Bella coming?"

"Half an hour ago, or so they said."

The fire catches and Horia stands up, grimacing as he rubs his lower back. His hair, eyebrows, and clothes are flecked with fine, grey powder. It looks like cement dust. I ask how we'll make *palinca*. He points at a big copper pot that sits inside the drum.

"This is the still. I've put my fermented fruit inside. The fire will heat it from below, see? When the fruit boils, the steam goes up the funnel into the copper pipe and across there, to the second drum. Come and see what happens in that one."

We walk to the second drum. It has no lid and is full of water, cold to the touch. The horizontal pipe from the first drum enters this one and snakes down through the water in a wide spiral, then exits through the drum wall, low down. Pipe and drum have been welded at that point so water cannot leak.

"See how it works?" says Horia.

"Almost. But why does this pipe circle round and round?"

"So it goes through as much cold water as possible."

"Right. To maximise the wotsit, the cooling of the steam?"

"Distillation, correct." Horia points at an enamel bowl on the grass alongside the second drum, directly under the protruding end of the copper pipe. "And can you guess what the bowl is for?"

"To catch the *palinca?*"

He gives me a mischievous grin. "Correct, but, actually, we'll get *palinca* only after the second distillation. The first distillation gives us *țuica.* It depends which you prefer. Anyway, you'll see."

"Can't wait. We don't make this in England."

"What do you make?"

"Tea, mostly, in a pot. But *this?* This is something else." I stand back to admire the set-up. It's simple enough but well put together.

"Domnul Mike."

"Yes?"

"Stop daydreaming. A fire needs fuel." Horia points to a pile of scrap wood: *Fetch.* I crouch down, grab a few chunks and shove them into the smoking hole at the bottom of the first drum.

"Good," says Horia, "not too much and not too little. We want a steady heat, OK? Not enough heat means my fruit won't boil. Too much heat means my still will blow up, which means no *palinca,* and no more Domnul Mike. So, be careful. I'll be back soon."

"Thanks for the tip. Steady heat. Where are you going?"

"To do something else."

He tramps uphill, poking at his phone. His green wellies suck at his shins and beady-eyed hens scatter before him.

I add a bit more wood to the smouldering recess, then take some out, just in case. We want a steady heat. Not Chernobyl.

Horia's short and stocky neighbours arrive an hour late. *Bună, Mike!* Vlad wears a blue tracksuit with a

Chelsea FC badge and faded yellow espadrilles. His wife wears a black sequinned top, tight black jeans, and lots of eye-liner. Her pony-tail bobs about as she walks. Bella looks good for her age, with a bright smile, and a deep, weathered tan from working outdoors, rain or shine.

They're lugging a plastic tub – fifty litres or so – with handles that protrude like ears. They position it in front of mine, closer to the still, presumably because those who came last shall be next. Vlad jabs a stubby finger at the fire. "Wood, Mike."

I add some more.

"Not that much," says Bella, and I pull some out.

Vlad removes the lid from my tub and sniffs my fruity goop.

"God help us. What are you making, after-shave?" He wipes his eyes, for effect, and makes a face: *Aaargh.*

Bella takes a whiff. "Quite nice, actually, sort of exotic."

"Sort of *Old Spice*," says Vlad.

I point at the fire. "Enough wood?"

Vlad sucks his teeth. "Far too much. The still is gonna blow."

"What?" I take a step back.

Bella laughs. "He's teasing you, Mike. I'll seal the cracks."

"The cracks?"

"Watch and learn," says Vlad.

Bella opens her knapsack and takes out a pack of flour, a small ceramic mug, and a spoon. She puts a few heaped spoonfuls of flour into the mug, adds water, and mixes a thick paste. She applies the paste, by hand, to the edges of the copper funnel at the top of the drum where it meets the horizontal pipe. Within minutes, the heat from the copper has dried the paste to a thick, white crust. I watch and learn, dead impressed.

"Nice pastry, Bella. Who taught you that trick?"

"My grandma, ages ago. I'd get such blisters doing it as a kid, but not these days. Plenty of practise, see. We make *palinca* every year, sometimes twice, depending on how much fruit we get from our trees. *Asta e.*"

That's how it is, and long may it be so.

I'm sitting on a tree stump near the copper still and reading my Kindle – somewhat surprised to learn what utter failures most of the Nazi leaders were before they became Nazi leaders – when I hear the first *ping.* It sounds like an alert on someone's phone, but Vlad and Bella are up at Horia's place doing something else and there's no one here but us chickens. *Ping, ping.* There it goes again. I rise from my stump, glancing about. *What is that?* The noise is coming from the water-filled drum. I look closer. Clear liquid drips from the pipe into the bowl. *Ping, ping, ping.*

I call Horia's number, pronto. "Horia, time to try your *palinca*."

"Too busy. You try it, use the little glass. I'll be down later."

He's gone before you can say, *What little glass?* I find it on a wooden shelf under the hen house and collect drops of hooch. *Sip sip.* It tastes of apple but contains very little alcohol. *How come?* As far as I know, *palinca* is about forty percent alcohol. Then again, what do I know – that's probably after the second distillation?

I crouch and wait, watching the drips and feeling like a proper one. Soon, there's a continuous dribble and I try again. This time, the flavour is more complex and kicks like a nervous horse, straight to the head. *Wow.* It reminds me of the first time I tasted *calvados*, as a pimply teenager, on a school trip to France. But that was then. Right now, we need a steady heat. And maybe I should sample a little more hooch, while I wait for Horia and the others. Scientific research, and so on.

Horia comes trotting downhill, belly bouncing. Vlad and Bella are right behind him. They all try the hooch and seem pleased. Presumably, they've tasted better and worse. Vlad holds the little glass up to the light.

"See that, Domnul Mike? Clean and natural."

Horia sips. "So far, so good. But keep that fire steady, Mike, and never mind your book, or whatever that thing is." He points at my Kindle. I should not be reading; I should be kindling. Horia strides uphill towards his house. To do something else.

"What's keeping him so busy?" I ask.

"Concrete," says Vlad.

"And you're helping?"

"I was, but now I'll stay here and do the gravel."

"For the concrete?"

"No, for the still."

Vlad dons a pair of old gloves, removes the hot funnel from the top of the copper still and sets it on the ground. Next, he grabs a long-handled spade, scoops mucky gravel from the path and empties it into the gaping mouth of the still. *Watch and learn?* I gawp and wonder. *What's he up to?* Sabotage, perhaps.

"Clean and natural, eh, Vlad?"

"Well, if we don't add gravel, the fruit will stick to the bottom and burn. Then, the *palinca* will taste of smoke. Not good, Mike."

"But what about germs?"

"What about 'em? Do you know how hot it gets, inside that still? Bye-bye, germs."

Horia's fermented apples produce ten litres of hooch, which Bella and I pour into a demijohn. Wearing his old gloves, Vlad scoops steaming mush from the still, using an empty old paint pot, and plops it in a wooden trough. "Lambs love eating this, Mike."

"No wonder they jump about."

When the still is empty, Bella carefully pours the first distillation back into the copper pot, and I add wood below it.

After a little while, drips are *ping-ping-pinging* once again into the enamel bowl. When it's half full, Bella takes a little coloured stick about the size of a cigarette from her knapsack and places it into the liquid. The stick bobs about like an angler's float, but it has lines and numbers along its edge like a thermometer.

"To measure alcohol content," says Bella, before I can ask.

"Clever. Because the strength changes, right?"

"Right. *Palinca* starts weak, gets stronger, then goes weak again." Bella beckons me closer and points at the little stick in the bowl. "We're at forty-seven, see? Percent, I mean. Horia wants forty, so when the *palinca* dilutes down to that, we're done."

"But won't the pipe keep dripping?"

"Yes, and we save the rest in a different bowl. Then, we add it to the next batch."

"Right. How does that little stick work, by the way?"

"This? Chemicals, look." Bella lifts the coloured float from the bowl and holds it up. At the bottom end of the stick is a small glass bulb containing a finely-granulated powder. *Chemicals, see?*

I'm baffled. "It can measure alcohol content through glass?"

Bella shrugs and places the float back into the bowl of *palinca*. "No idea, Mike. It's quite a new invention, for us folks at least."

"But, without one of those, how did your grandma measure alcohol in her *palinca,* all those years ago?"

"She'd just keep trying it until she was happy." Bella grins up at me and her mascara'd eyes twinkle in sunshine. She turns back to the magic float, head cocked to read it. "Forty-four, love."

Vlad inverts his thumb like a bored Caesar. "No good."

"Give it time."

"I'm just saying."

"Tell you what," says Bella, "our flow seems slow. How's that water doing, can you check?" She points at the second oil drum.

Vlad dips his fingers into it. "Too warm. I'll add some cold."

He walks to a standpipe, fills a bucket with water, and pours it into the second drum. The warm water inside brims over and dribbles down the outside. After half a dozen bucketfuls, Vlad dips a finger into the drum – testing, testing. "Cold now, that'll do it."

Sure enough, the flow of *palinca* increases, *drip-drip-drip* into the enamel bowl. "Your turn soon, Mike," says Bella.

"But we're next," says Vlad, rubbing his palms together.

By mid-afternoon, the sky is overcast, my eyes sting from woodsmoke, and my head is tight from scientific research. Tastes like heaven, this moonshine, but it can give you a hell of a hangover. I learned that the hard way in 1994, during my first visit to this enchanted, enervating land. Those were the daze. Work hard, play hard, and pass the Paracetamol.

Vlad offers me a little glass. "Here you go, try mine. Plums."

I try to look enthusiastic, as I sip. "Yeah, tastes good."

"Now it's your turn. Ready to rock?"

"Let's do it."

Vlad empties the plum mash, Bella mixes her paste, and I haul my Tub Tropicana across the grass towards the copper still.

An hour later, I'm sniffing the second distillation in the enamel bowl. *Bananas?* Smells like victory. I'm making *palinca*. Vlad and Bella come to investigate. She tries it first.

"Tastes of pineapple. Did you put pineapple in this, Mike?"

"All sorts."

"Certainly different. I feel as if I'm on holiday, somewhere far away." Bella passes me the glass. "You try."

My *palinca* smells like perfume but tastes OK, if you like drinking *Poison* by Dior, in a raspberry republic. Oddly enough, I do. Then I pass the glass on.

Vlad takes a sip and feigns a coughing fit. "God help us."

I peer into the glass. "Why is my *palinca* cloudy, not clear?"

"It'll clear in time," says Vlad, "give it a month in the dark."

"Looks a bit oily too, how come?"

"That'll be the kiwi," says Bella. "Nice enough, though."

"You reckon?"

"Well, we've never tasted *palinca* like this," says Vlad.

"Is that a good thing?"

"It's not a bad thing."

Bella crouches beside the bowl and raises her float.

"Forty?"

I raise a thumb, as you do.

My tub produces eight litres of fragrant *palinca* that tastes of any fruit you care to mention, plus carrot. We're all done.

"Time I got home. Thanks for your help, this is for you."

I hand Vlad a two-litre plastic bottle of my tropical hooch then walk up to Horia's house and give him a bottle, too. Horia takes a sip and nudges my arm.

"Robinson Crusoe, you are."

He'll probably tell the whole village, as no man is an island.

"Thanks for letting me use your still, Horia. I learned a lot."

"Pleasure. Want to see my concrete?"

"Love to."

"Follow me, mind your head."

"Bit late for that."

He leads me to his stinky brick hut, where we admire a rectangle of wet concrete, one metre by two, just big enough for a pig not to turn around in. Vertical iron bars are kept in place by a lattice of horizontal wooden beams, presumably until the concrete dries. Then Horia will add a door, with a padlock, I expect.

"Nice work. Where's your lucky pig?"

"Outside, Domnul Mike."

"Outside?"

"Look though this hole, you might see him."

I peep through a slit in the brick wall and spot the pig in the field. He's bigger than last time and doing what pigs do best – waddling here, nosing there. Long may he grunt.

"But won't he dig up your garden, Horia?"

"A bit, but I reckon he's happier. Or so I heard."

"Good for you. And for him. Now, I'll be off."

"Let's drink a little glass before you go."

"No way, I've got to get my little jeep up your big hill."

"So what? There's never any cops."

"It's not the cops I'm worried about, it's the trees."

I drive home, extra slowly, listening to Muddy Waters singing *Hoochie Coochie Man*. He's got seven hundred dollars. And I've got four litres of fruity *palinca*. Don't you mess with me.

Angela and I sit on our terrace, facing the stark ridge of mountains. It's getting chilly out here, but I have something to warm our cockles. I fetch two shot glasses and fill them up.

"Interesting aroma," says Angela. "Was it hard work?"

"Yes and no. My job was to keep the fire steady."

"You smell of smoke. You know it's illegal to make *palinca?*"

"Only if you sell it, apparently."

"It's illegal, full stop."

"Now you tell me? So, how come almost every family in Romania keeps a bottle of *palinca* stashed in a cupboard?"

"Because we've been doing it for hundreds of years."

"Illegally?"

"No, that's only since we joined the EU."

"Better drink up. Before some Brussels sprout locks us up."

Angela swirls her glass. "Smells of oranges, like Cointreau."

"Not to mention bananas."

"You said it, Mike."

"Well?"

"Well what?"

"Are you going to try our hooch?"

"Yes, I'm just admiring the view, savouring the moment."

We gaze at green slopes, gentle hills, and mountains that soar into a pink and purple sky. Then we clink our glasses.

"To Palincashire."

"Palincashire."

Uncle Nelu

Uncle Nelu steps with some difficulty from the train. Angela and I move quickly along the platform, side-stepping other passengers to greet him. He's frail but looks as dapper as ever, toting an elegant overnight bag made from beige suede, with red straps.

Small, lean, and tanned, Nelu is smiling despite a seven-hour trip. He wears his silver hair long and tucked behind his pixie ears. His silver beard is neatly clipped to a rattish point. And such clothes – Panama hat, lime-green Nike trainers, and a New York Yankees wind-cheater. For his age, Uncle Nelu is street style on legs. He shuffles up, seventy years young, extending his arms.

"Angela, come here."

They hug and peck. Then it's my turn. Nelu takes my face in his little brown hands and kisses me on both cheeks, *mwah*. He smells of cologne. What a gentleman. Cologne and cigarettes.

I carry his bag and compliment him on his appearance. Nelu tells me that his two kids in America send him the latest fashions.

"Mara bought me these. Very comfortable." He glances down at his rather large, luminous trainers. He's not the only one.

On the drive to our home in the mountains, Nelu doesn't say much. He sits in the back, apparently happy just looking across green plains towards the soaring peaks. It's a spectacular view and most of our visitors would say, *Wow*. But not this one. I catch his eye in the rear-view mirror.

"What are you thinking, Nelu?"

"Couldn't live in these mountains. Not for long, anyway."

"So, one weekend should be plenty," says Angela.

"No problem, my girl, all I need is a television."

Angela glances at me. I shrug. *Over to you, I'm driving.*

"Uncle Nelu," says Angela, "something you should know…"

As she explains, I watch Nelu in the mirror. He looks as if he's just been told he has three days to live. Without a television.

Nelu disembarks in our yard, lights a cigarette, and stands gawking at the jagged ridge of mountains. Our dogs circle and sniff the stranger. He seems wary, at first, but eventually, he pats their heads. The dogs wag their tails and, introductions over, trot away to bark at a donkey in the lane. *Bugger off, Big Ears.*

Nelu watches then turns back to the mountains. With his long silver hair and beard, he looks like Moses who just came down. I wonder what he's thinking.

Thou shalt be bored out of thy skull.

"Didn't you tell Nelu, when you asked him to house-sit?"

"It never occurred to me," says Angela, peeling a carrot.

"Poor Nelu, no TV." I glance through the window at the terrace, where Nelu is sipping beer and exhaling smoke – or perhaps it's coming from his ears. "Is he angry?"

Angela shrugs. "Disappointed, certainly. But he'll get over it. He's the same with his wife – everything has to be perfect."

"Poor Auntie Beti. You should have invited her, instead."

"She'd love to house-sit for us but she has an ailing mum to look after. As well as Nelu. Could you fetch me two big onions, please?"

I go outside, get a trowel, and plod downhill to the vegetable patch. Nelu is still on the terrace. I can't see him, because of a helpful tree, but I can hear him. He's on the phone to his wife.

"No, Beti, I didn't bring my radio. How was I to know?"

Oh, well. Nelu can borrow ours. Angela can tell him.

She opens the lid of our big freezer in the garage and shows Nelu what's inside.

"Help yourself while we're away. Plenty of frozen fishy things, pizzas, garlic bread, all sorts. How are you with cooking?"

"I'm not. Beti does the cooking. I do other things."

"That's pretty much what Beti told me, but no problem, just pick what you fancy and read the instructions on the packet."

"Any meat?"

"Actually, yes, I bought some specially for you. Here, see?"

Nelu eyes a pack of frozen chicken legs and a steak pie. Angela points across the garage. "In that little fridge, you have salami from Sibiu. The lady in the shop told me it's a good one."

"You people don't eat meat?"

"No, we don't." Angela points into the freezer again. "Vanilla ice-cream, chocolate ice-cream, and some orange sorbet, ок?"

Nelu looks worried. "Orange *what?*"

"Sorbet. It's like ice-cream."

"So why don't you just say *ice-cream,* same as everyone else?"

Angela closes the freezer with a gentle thud, and we move on. I nudge Nelu's elbow. He gives me the eye. *What now?* I point at the booze shelf, where bottles of my best tropical brew shimmer in the neon light. "You like *palinca,* Nelu?"

"*Palinca?* Who doesn't? I make mine from plums, the best plums. I invest in the best and I get the best."

"Sounds good. I make *palinca,* too. It's got bananas in it."

Nelu's eyebrows go north and my stock goes south.

Angela serves us a delicious dinner – *parmigiana,* garlic bread, and a crispy green salad with a tasty dressing. Uncle Nelu pokes at his food, glum-faced. Angela goes out to the garage and returns with a salami. Nelu shaves a few slices onto his plate and seems in better spirits. Or maybe it's the wine. After dinner, he smokes on the terrace and is in bed by eight.

"He's from the countryside," says Angela, as I wash up.

I scrub a pot and look through our window at the fields, valleys, and mountains. I'd like to think Uncle Nelu feels at home here, but I doubt it somehow.

We drive away early next morning. Our dogs stand whining through the fence. Nelu stands with a ciggie on his lips, fiddling with our radio. He looks tired and rather peeved.

"He was up at 4 a.m.," says Angela.

"Doing what?"

"Other things."

Our long weekend at the Transylvanian Book Festival proves very enjoyable. A cosy and inspiring event, it's held in a sleepy little village and attended by fifty or so bookworms, most of whom are upper-middle class Brits and frightfully well-to-do. Talk about posh. I mention this over dinner to the glamorous, middle-aged Englishwoman on my left, and she pats my arm.

"We're not *posh,* we just have silly voices. And, may I say, dear Mayk, I did so enjoy your super talk, this efternune."

If she's not posh, I'm Prince Charles.

The highlight of our stay is a cultural evening in the grounds of a fortified church – chapel meets castle, sort of thing. Transylvania has many examples, each magnificent and alluring in its own way. At this one, we sit on the ramparts, leaning back against a stone wall one metre thick. We peep through the slits for firing arrows and down holes for pouring hot oil. But there's no siege tonight. Just sweet words and music.

Two poets – one Romanian, one Scot – recite sonnets by Shakespeare, in English first then in translation. Next, we listen to classical music played on harpsichord and two violins. Bliss.

The clear sky is cobalt blue and dotted with just a few stars. The full moon dazzles my eyes and the cool air of early autumn is balm for the soul. I take my wife's hand. We've been together twenty years and worked our way around a risky world, but Transylvania is home. Peace and plenty. Some nice people. Good times. Life doesn't get any better. Then her phone rings.

Heads turn and Angela scurries quickly away, like a maid fleeing medieval mayhem. I rise and follow. We slip down wooden stairs and through an arch into an empty courtyard, where pigeons peck at clipped grass. Angela cups a hand to her ear. "Uncle, are you ок?" She glances at me. "He's afraid of the dogs."

"Why, have they escaped and got in a fight? Attacked that donkey?"

"No idea, but he sounds stressed. Line was breaking up."

"Put him on speaker, so I can hear."

Angela pokes at her phone and Nelu's voice crackles at us. "Angela, I repeat, where-is-your-microwave?"

"We don't have one, Uncle Nelu. Tell me about the dogs."

"As I said, I fed the dogs. Now, I'm trying to feed me."

"Oh, I see. Why do you need a microwave?"

"I'm cooking those frozen fishy things. What a palaver."

"Are you following the instructions on the packet?"

"Of course. Bake 'em, fry 'em, then microwave 'em."

"Uncle Nelu, you're supposed to choose just one."

"One what?"

"Method. You bake them, or fry them, or microwave them."

"Oh."

"Have you fried them?"

"Yes, after I baked 'em."

"How are they looking?"

"Not like on the packet. When are you back?"

"Tomorrow afternoon."

"About time."

"Anything you need? Something I can pick up on the way?"

"A television."

Marvellous Market

"Hmm, how about this one?" says the ruddy-faced shepherd, offering me an astrakhan hat the size of a pedal bin.

I have a large head, you see, albeit not filled with brains. The shepherd leans towards me, across his market stall, all smiles, waiting. He reaches for a little cracked mirror and holds it up, urging me on. I look in the mirror and see a man wearing an astrakhan hat. It's me. At least, the latest version.

"Yes, this one fits, thanks. How much?"

I flip open my wallet. The shepherd peeps in. We agree on a price that pleases him and stings me, but I probably deserve it. I stroll away from his stall, with a toasty head and a raging conscience. *What a hypocrite, buying an astrakhan hat made from the wool of unborn lambs black as soot?* I feel bad. But I also feel warm, and, up here in the mountains of Transylvania, when winter comes a-howling and the mercury plunges to minus 30°C, I'll be grateful, because real fleece trumps the synthetic stuff, any day of the weeklong blizzard. *Yours sincerely, A. Vegetarian.* That's the tricky part. These are my principles and if you don't like them, I have others. Groucho Marx said that.

I walk across the busy market square. Must be about a thousand people here, gathered around stalls and food vendors, under the shadow of Bran Castle with its ancient pointy roof, medieval walls, and modern prices of admission. The blurb up there pushes the 'Dracula' angle, but if you believe that, you'll believe any trinket. My brother visited the castle last summer. No gullible tourist, he emerged blinking an hour later and said, "More confused than before I went in."

Tired-eyed women bulge under layers of black clothing and beckon me to examine their wares: brass cowbells, old bayonets, tacky plastic toys, leather saddles, leather bridles, and heavy-looking, hand-tooled leather belts that droop from a sturdy hook. The belts are one centimetre thick and ten centimetres wide. You might as well wear a saddle. The women wiggle their podgy fingers at me. *Come!* I wiggle fingers at them and back off, because as President Putin might say, *Tanks but no tanks*.

The sun glints through November clouds, and steam bellows from a huge grill of sweaty little sausages. *Meat?* Never touch the stuff, myself. Not for the last thirty-five years. Never will again. If St Peter is a vegetarian, perhaps I'll get into heaven. But if the Lamb of God is gambolling around the Pearly Gates, I'll probably go to hell. In this hat.

"Domnul, you need a jumper, try one of mine, hand-knitted!" A middle-aged woman with irresistible blue eyes calls to me from behind her stall. How can she see under my coat? She must have X-ray vision like a Marvel superhero. Marvel superheroine, rather. *Woolly Jumper Woman.* For it is she.

I peruse her wares and try to look as if I know a thing or three about knitwear. The jumpers are beige with

V-necks. *Hand-knitted?* Doubt it; they all look the same. I slip off my coat, and try one on. It's good and warm, thick and heavy. The last time I wore something this heavy, it was bulletproof. I feel like Ned Kelly. *Come and have a go if you think you're kangaroo enough.* Perhaps this is Transylvanian Kevlar, resistant to gamma rays. Whatever, it matches my new hat. I look like a local yokel.

"Oh, yes, my love." The woman beams at me like a favourite aunt who rarely visits and brings things that don't fit. "Perfect."

"You don't say."

"Take a look." She brandishes a mirror and I peep in. *Wow, good news, I have shoulders like Ben Affleck.* Maybe I'll buy it, after all. Or maybe I won't. Warm but rather rectangular.

"These shoulders, Doamna, they seem a bit boxy to me?"

"It's been on a hanger, Domnul."

On Dr Frankenstein's monster, more like. "How much?"

"Two hundred, Domnul. Handmade, you see."

"On a machine, from what I see?"

"Yes, handmade on a machine. How about one seventy-five?"

"How about one-fifty?"

"All right, seeing as it's you."

Seeing as we've never met before, I pay up and stride away wearing my magic top. People gasp. *It's Woolly Jumper Man.*

Next stop, a stall attended by two shepherds wearing huge, fluffy beige capes made from sheep fleeces. They're sitting on stools and look like bored polar bears. They sip at plastic cups, to cheer their spirits, no doubt. I ask if I may take a photo. They rise, strike a pose, and tell me it takes five sheep to make one *sarica*. Clever sheep, should be on *Bran's Got Talent*.

The taller shepherd unhooks his cape. "Try my *sarica*, Domnul? Very good for the hills. We sleep outside, in these."

"I bet you do. But I'm not a shepherd. Thanks, all the same."

"American?"

"English."

"You could wear it in London to meet the Queen."

"I'd probably get arrested." I point at a dark, sleeveless something lined with curly, white fleece and drooping from a rusty nail on the plank behind them.

"Is that a waistcoat?"

The small man reaches for it. "Yes, it's a *bunda*. Here, try."

The *bunda* weighs several kilos and is a remarkable piece of tailoring, made from dark brown needlecord. Rough and rugged, it is hand-sewn with black leather trim. The fleece lining is thick, soft and warm to the touch, but the *bunda* looks a bit small. I ask for a bigger size. The shepherds shake their heads.

"I only made that one," says the tallest fellow. "Took me ages, hardly worth my time. Anyway, they're meant to be snug. Try it, and tell me I'm wrong."

I remove my jumper and slip into something a little more *bunda*. The shorter shepherd nods. "Perfect fit, Domnul."

"You won't find better," says his companion, sipping hooch.

"But this *bunda* doesn't have any buttons," I say.

"We couldn't find big ones."

"You could sew some on, Domnul. Can you sew?"

"Yes, but not as well as you can. You made this yourself?"

They both nod, presumably because success has many fathers whereas failure is an orphan. Either way, this *bunda* needs a home, and I'm smitten. They want forty lei. I give them fifty, and ask if I can post my photo of them on Facebook.

The shepherds exchange worried glances. *Do what to us?*

Wandering around the stalls, I spot a familiar face from our village. It's Domnul Abel, dressed in his Sunday best: dark suit, dark hat, bloodstain on his collar. He shakes my hand vigorously, as though I'm a long-lost debtor. I treat him to a glass of *palinca* from a stall. Not that he needs it. Abel reeks of booze and wants to tell me secrets, mostly those of our neighbours, some of whom he dislikes.

"May a thousand horses trample them," Abel says, raising his glass and almost tripping over his feet. His shoelaces are undone, and he will be, too, if he doesn't slow down. He rambles on, hissing his colourful harangue. He'd make a charming baddie. *Palinca Man.*

Angela turns up, laden down with goodies. *Wonder Wife.* I spy green leeks and a jar of glimmering honey in one of her bags. I pass her my heavy waistcoat and she nods approvingly.

"Nice *bunda*. Where are the buttons?"

"I'll sew some on. You like my jumper?"

Angela steps back to appraise it. "Weird shoulders. You look like a robot."

"It's been on a hanger. Like my astrakhan hat?"

"Very warm, I bet. May I see?"

I take it off and Angela tries it on. Suits her, very rural, very authentic, very Transylvania.

Palinca Man moves closer. "Buy one, Doamna Angela, you won't regret it."

"Perhaps, Abel." Angela caresses the shiny, black, rippled wool. "But these hats are made from baby lambs, aren't they?"

She looks me in the eye, and I can't deny it.

Run for Your Life

"Want to watch me run a race, Domnul Mike?"

Bogdan peeps through our fence, his dark eyes glinting in the autumn sun. He's a good-looking adolescent but seems troubled. Before I can answer, he kicks a stone and complains that *nobody* ever comes to see him race. *Parents? Elder sister?* Forget it.

"They're always busy. How about you, Domnul?"

I lean on my garden rake and ask Bogdan for more details, buying myself some time until Angela joins me at the fence. She's carrying a bucket of mucky red onions from our vegetable patch. Bogdan repeats his litany of woe. Angela listens with interest, then turns to me, and says, "I've just had an idea. We could film him."

"Film who?" says Bogdan, and we explain. *You, Domnul.*

Come race day, Bogdan is perched in the back of our jeep, pointing directions. *Next left.* He wears a tracksuit and running shoes. No bag, no bottle of water. Travel light.

Angela is in the passenger seat, pointing her camera back at Bogdan. She adjusts the clip mic on his top and interviews him about his training routine, which sounds Olympic for a thirteen-year-old. He seems preoccupied, even worried.

"I'll probably lose. National event today, lots of competition."

I catch his eye in my rear-view mirror. "Think positive, Bogdan. A cross-country race is like nuclear war – it's not winning that counts, it's taking part."

"Right." He looks even more worried, but not for long. "Hey, Doamna Angela, did you say I'll be on TV?"

"On YouTube," Angela replies. "We're making some short documentaries about village life. You'll be in one."

"Oh, right."

We park in a gravel yard, alongside a little lawn with a memorial to the First World War, to await Bogdan's colleagues. We climb out to inspect artillery cannons used in a military campaign in 1916. Dew glistens on the grass around an information placard. We pause to read it. Seems the German army took the Romanians by surprise in these mountains. Hell of a scrap, too, and part of the ferocious Battle of Transylvania. I point at names engraved on a marble slab. The fallen are pushing up our daisies. It makes you think.

"How do you feel about all this, Bogdan?"

"They paid the ultimate sacrifice and we are grateful."

He's reading verbatim from the slab and looks troubled.

The hills are alive with yells and screams: *Faster! They're right behind you!* Spindly teenagers – boys and girls in staggered heats – puff and pant along a winding, two-kilometre course. The terrain is steep and rough. Their teammates urge them on. We yell for Bogdan. Angela clutches her camera, panning and zooming. It's fun. At least for us.

A hundred years ago, almost to the day, right here, terrified lads ran for their lives, or towards their deaths. Some paid the ultimate sacrifice. Today, we don't even have to pay a parking fee.

Bogdan wins his race. He's a hero. Immortal. Collapses in a heap, breathing hard. I offer a banana from my bag. He wolfs it down. Agrees to an interview. *In a minute.*

A hundred yards from home, we meet his parents. Bella and Vlad have scythes over their shoulders, sweat on their brows, and awkward grins. Bogdan leans from our car and tells his mum, *When someone shouts your name, it fills your heart.* His dad says they'll come next time. *Promise.* Bogdan sits back and tells me, *Drive on*. I salute him in my mirror.

Job done. And a nice day out, all told. The past met the present met the future, as so often up here. It's one of the things I love about Transylvania. So, drop in, you might live forever.

No Business like Snow Business

"Perfect weather for a long drive."

I turn the ignition key, glancing through our windscreen. Above us only sky, blue and beautiful. The sun has got his Ray Bans on. Not bad for a late November afternoon. Transylvania, here we come.

My wife buckles her seat belt. "Four hours and two hundred kilometres to go, fingers crossed."

"And toes. We were lucky on the drive down, this morning. So maybe we'll be lucky on our way home, this afternoon. Your turn to pick a CD."

Angela selects the music and we're soon cruising across big and busy Bucharest, listening to the modern, elegiac klezmer of Yiddish Art Trio. Or rather, we're listening to this city's honking horn section and crawling along in bonkers traffic. First sign of a gap, a yellow Dacia taxi cuts in front of us; its bumper sticker says *Welcome to Bucharest*. Will things ever change, here? Probably not.

I picture our tranquil little village tucked between soaring peaks. Home sweet home. We'll be there by nightfall, with luck. Tomorrow nightfall, at this rate.

Judging by the jams ahead, we'll need an hour to get out of Dodge.

"Nice bass." Angela boosts the volume on the CD.

"Benjy Fox-Rosen, very talented."

"How do you remember so many names?"

"Like you remember numbers and directions. I just do."

"Left at the roundabout, Mike, then middle lane."

"You see?"

"I see clouds, in the distance."

She's right about that, too, and there they are.

On the *autostrada* the speed limit is 130 kph, so things move faster. A lot faster, for some people. An open-top, red Lamborghini zooms past us. The bearded driver looks about twenty-five. His car resembles a toy and is soon a red smudge in the distance. I wonder if that lad is truly rich, as in big-villa-on-sea, or the sort who lives in a tiny flat and spends his life's savings on a fast car, because that's what life is about? Whatever, I hope he's wearing a seat belt. I glance at my watch. Three hours to go. Nice and easy.

Angela points at a sign. "Services, I need a loo."

"Me too."

I pull in and we step out. The air is surprisingly cold. We're at a higher altitude. Sky's changing too, grimy grey now. The sun seems to have vanished. By 5 p.m.? See you later, alligator.

The service station is quiet and the queues are short, so I'm soon back in the car, rummaging through our CDs. It's time for some African music. *The Four Brothers* boom from the speakers, all sun and sparkle. But when

I look up, it's raining in the car park. Actually, it's snowing, or something in between. *Baba Iarna* is coming.

Angela scoots back into the car, brushing crystallized droplets of water from her jumper. "What do you call this yukky stuff, in English?"

I gaze out. "This? This is manky sleet."

"A big blob of it went right down the back of my neck. If we've got manky sleet here, what's waiting for us in the mountains?"

"True. We'd better get a move on."

"But don't drive fast, Mike."

"Couldn't if I tried. Seen the traffic jam, ahead? More lights than Las Vegas."

"Good. You want a doughnut?"

We munch, and our wheels crunch. Getting icy, too. *Great!*

The traffic jam stretches ten kilometres and takes an hour to unwind. At the end of it, a lone traffic cop stands at a tricky intersection, gesturing at drivers coming from three different directions. There are no traffic lights, it's just another of Romania's bizarre junctions that seem intended to cause accidents rather than prevent them. Whoever designed this one should be locked up, in a car, in winter, no CDs, no doughnuts, throw away the key. That's what I'd do. As for our cop, he's doing his best, chin tucked into his parka, poor sod. We inch past, nodding gratitude. *Is that an icicle under his nose?*

If the hills were tricky, the mountains are treacherous and we're soon driving in a blizzard on a winding road through dense forest. Fat snowflakes whip across our windscreen. Visibility is poor. Our car is big, comfy, and four-wheel drive, but finds these conditions difficult. Our back-end skids on some of the hairpin bends.

"Sliding, again," says Angela.

"Icy and dicey, out there."

"Hope we don't get stranded. Did you bring a proper coat?"

"Just this tweed jacket."

"Woolly sweater? Hat? Gloves?"

"*Niet,* as they say in Siberia."

"Boots?"

"Nope. Weather forecast said *sunny day,* this morning."

"It's November and you're in canvas pumps?"

"Converse All Star, if you don't mind."

"Right, that should help. What were you thinking?"

"That we'd drive to Bucharest and drive back, nice and easy. I listened to the weather girl. On the radio. In our kitchen."

"And you believed her."

"I'll take that radio back to the shop, ask for a refund."

Angela's phone rings, and I catch a familiar voice on the line. It's Uncle Nelu, our house-sitter for the day. He mentions *viscol.* Means blizzard, I think. Word is getting around. Maybe he heard it on TV, his favourite place. I hope he's enjoying the one we bought especially for him, back home.

Angela reassures her uncle that we're doing fine, just as an articulated lorry lumbers around a steep bend above us and jackknifes into our lane. *Yikes.* The huge trailer is lurching down on us. *WTF?* I squeeze the brakes so we don't slip into the maw of the slithering, steel monster. The lorry settles into a straight line and the headlights wink at us – *cheers* – as it roars past. Good driver but what a job. I wouldn't send a dog out on a night like this, never mind a trucker. I wish I were home, watching Formula 1.

We're heading downhill again. This is easier, in some respects, except every time I apply the brakes, I hear them suck and chew on a potentially-lethal cocktail of snow, slush, and ice. *What if the wheels jam?* We'll ski-doo into the vast, dark forest, is what. I just hope the bears are well fed and fast asleep.

Fixing my gaze on the red tail-light of a motorcycle, I follow it around bend after bend – blind believer that I am. Was this how the Three Wise Men felt, tracking a solitary star to their salvation, one December night, two thousand years ago? Makes you think. *Oh well, Christmas soon.* I do love Christmas. All that goodwill, plus new socks. Not to mention sherry for Santa. He'll find your chimney even if you haven't got one. Christmas carols too, I can't wait. When I was a good little scallywag, we'd improvise and sing our own:

> *We three men, from Orient are,*
> *One in a bus and one in a car,*
> *One on a scooter, beeping his hooter,*
> *Followed by Ringo Starr.*

Funny at the time, I suppose. These days, how many kids have heard of Ringo? Not many, I bet, but I hope they will, some day. Cracking little drummer boy. Played in a decent band, too.

Angela pockets her phone. "I told Nelu not to worry and we'll be in touch. He said you should stop singing and concentrate on the road. Because he used to be a driver and he should know."

"And so on."

"Nice tune, by the way."

"Just some Christmas carol. Did you sing carols at school?"

"No, only in Grandma's village. Her neighbours would give us walnuts. Me and my sisters would get about four hundred each."

"Four hundred walnuts? How did you carry them?"

"In a sack hung around our necks. It's called *traista*."

"Didn't you get money, or sweets?"

"Just nuts. We were happy enough. Did you go around the houses and sing carols?"

"That only happened on Christmas cards. Sing carols in our street, people would think you *were* nuts. Can you believe this bloody blizzard?"

"Code Yellow tonight, Nelu told me."

"What does that mean, again?"

"It means *be aware*, because severe weather might come."

"Already has. What's next, Code Igloo?"

We peer into swirling snow; sunny Bucharest seems long ago.

The road stretches away, shimmering white. I can hardly see through the veil of snowflakes but at least these bends are longer and gentler than those hairy hairpins.

A white van overtakes us, narrowly avoiding a head-on collision with a bus. *Nice work, White Van Man.* Then again, perhaps the driver was a woman. After all, the real point of gender equality is not that smart girls get to occupy top jobs usually reserved for smart boys, but that dim girls get to occupy jobs usually reserved for dim boys. *Anyway, good riddance, White Van Person.*

On the next strait, a lorry trundles towards us, flashing yellow hazard lights. As it passes, I spot a burly fellow standing in the back and wearing a fluorescent bib. He swings a spade from side to side, spattering the road – and our windscreen – with salty grit. Either he doesn't realise, or he doesn't care. The grit jams my wipers, allowing snowflakes to cover the windscreen within seconds. I turn a lever to apply a spurt of liquid cleaner, which creates a gritty, sleety soup that dribbles and grinds from left to right. Excellent. Perhaps those hazard lights mean *Idiot Onboard.*

The blizzard eases off, eventually, and visibility improves.

"We're through the worst. Code Pink and Fluffy, Angela?"

"I'll believe it when I'm sitting by our log fire."

"This is your captain speaking. One hour to touchdown."

"Let's try the radio, should be a news report on the hour."

We listen, with grim faces, to a traffic bulletin. It's a litany of accidents and emergency diversions. Code Chaos, out there.

We're cruising between three slow-moving lorries with identical markings that suggest a commercial convoy. There's something reassuring about it – I feel like a baby elephant in a herd of huge ones. The lorries are probably heading to Brașov, the city nearest to our home. So, we'll just coast along with them, until it's time for us to peel off and head into the mountains again. I glance at my watch. "We'll be home in forty-five minutes."

"Stay with these guys," says Angela, "I feel safe."

"Yuss, m'lady; very good, m'lady."

"Why the funny voice?"

"I'm imitating Parker, Lady Penelope's driver."

"Lady who?"

"Penelope, from *Thunderbirds*. You never saw *Thunderbirds?*"

Angela looks baffled and I realise, not for the first time, how many things she missed out on, as a youngster, when Romania's state TV broadcast only one or two hours per day and it was dismal communist propaganda at best. She prods my leg.

"Mike, tell me about your Lady Penelope."

"She was in *Thunderbirds,* a puppet show on TV, full colour. Essential viewing. Very modern, at the time. Sci-fi for kids."

"Never heard of it."

"And then there was *Captain Scarlet,* of course."

"Stay with these lorries."

"Yuss, m'lady."

Maybe I'll find *Thunderbirds* on YouTube when we get home and show Angela. Then again, maybe not. She might fancy Virgil.

We drive up steep bends through the forest, towards our village. The blizzard is back and blowing a gale. There's only one car on this perilous road, and we're in it. I do miss those big, wobbly lorries. Still, only seven kilometres to go. *Nice and easy, home soon.* Snowflakes dance pirouettes in the bright beams of our headlights and the ground is a silver carpet, three centimetres thick. To our left, the drifts lie deep and crisp and even. To our left, they slope sharply away into an abyss of majestic fir trees, thirty metres tall, branches laden white and drooping.

The higher we climb, the lower the temperature. Two minutes ago, the digital thermometer on our dashboard showed minus 6°C, now it's minus 8°C. Makes you wonder. How would it feel to be caught outside in a snowstorm? How long can our bodies tolerate deep snow and high wind? No idea. Countless individuals have perished in such weather, down the centuries. Blindsided by a blizzard. *What a way to go.*

"Not too fast on these hairbands, Mike."

"Hairpins."

"You know what I mean. These turns are dangerous."

"We'll be sipping mulled wine in ten minutes, you'll see."

Ten minutes later, we see snowdrifts. They curl from a rickety fence like the tails of a dozen giant white lizards that got stuck trying to climb through. The drifts are two metres apart and extend into the road. Still, we're on a downhill strait and crunching along at a decent pace. Two hundred metres from our front door. That's the good news. Now the weather.

A sudden, screaming wind sends great flurries of white across our path. My wipers are going like the clappers, but we seem to be driving through a plastic snow globe, our world turned upside down. I glimpse the drifts ahead. They look bigger now, somehow, and as we glide towards them, I floor the accelerator, just in case. The engine roars, and the car lurches on.

"Sit tight, Angela."

"Mike, slow down, those snowdrifts–"

We plough through the first two but the third is not so much lizard's tail as dinosaur's neck. The car grinds to a halt – wheels spinning, engine growling, all talk and no traction. *Six hours of driving and now this, a minute from home?* We're stuck. And it rhymes with the only word I can think of, as I turn off the engine.

"Fuck."

We sit and stare at dancing snowflakes. They seem happy enough, but we're up a creek without a clue.

"Well done," says Angela, "now what?"

The answer comes soon enough. We're standing in front of the car, teeth chattering in the wind. The road ahead is under half a metre of snow, and that's just the stretch we can see. The next bit, beyond the ridge, going down to our house, will probably be even worse, because it's more exposed and the drifts will be deeper. I turn towards my wife and yell into the blasting gale.

"Even if we could–"

Angela shakes her head. "We can't drive home!"

"So? Leave it here? Grab the bags and walk?"

Angela nods. Our stranded vehicle is blocking the road, but so are several tonnes of snow. No driver could go further. Game over.

We wade back towards the car, knee-deep in drifts, hands raised to shield our eyes against roaring clouds of white. I shout to Angela, "Can you believe this? It's like we're up Everest."

"Back inside, hurry."

We slither into warm seats. My forehead pounds and my ears hiss from the bitter wind. "My God, I was freezing out there."

"Not surprised, in those clothes. I'll phone Nelu with an update." Angela glances at her wing mirror. "Car coming."

I twist in my seat. Behind us, twin silver beams bob up and down like the lights of a small boat on a choppy sea. *Red car?* Yes, and I reckon I know who's driving it.

"I think it's Domnul Marin on his way home. No chance."

"I think he's beeping us to move, Mike."

"Can't he see we're bloody stuck?"

"Better get out and tell him. No way can he reach his yard tonight. He'll have to park back there. You should tell him."

"Will do. I may be some time, as Captain Oates said."

"Who's he, some puppet?"

"Never mind."

I clamber out and trudge uphill towards the headlights. Marin hops from his car. He's a dark-eyed, bearded little fellow in red overalls. We shake hands. I point at our car and explain. Marin listens, then yells that I must move our car because he'd like to park in his yard.

"Just down there, Domnul Mike, red door!"

He points. *Red door.* Perhaps he thinks I've forgotten, although we've been neighbours three years. He wants to park his red car outside his red door. He probably wears red pyjamas.

I peer down the lane, mulling over his daft suggestion. *Move our car?* I can hardly see our car in this damned blizzard. The snow is falling thick and fast.

The drifts are creeping higher by the nanosecond. My feet are turning to icy blocks. I need boots, gloves, a hat, an igloo. Marin flashes a warm smile, which helps.

"We'll use shovels, Domnul Mike!"

"Shovels? To do what?"

"Clear the snow, as far as my house. Then you'll drive down, park in my yard, and so can I. Why not?"

I blink in disbelief. Marin's place is thirty metres ahead of our car. *Clear the road?* It will take us an hour. He grins. Snowflakes buzz around us like a swarm of batty white bees. He points again.

"I've got a shovel, back in my car, Domnul Mike. Fetch yours, too."

"Mine's in my garage, Domnul Marin."

Now he's laughing, at me or with me. Either way, he looks demented, waving his arms as he plods back to his car. Perhaps I'm asleep, marooned in one of those nonsensical dreams. Yeah, I'll wake soon. Someone nudges my back. It's probably Angela urging me to get up.

Your turn to make the coffee, Mike.

I turn and see a woman. It's Doamna Jeni, the quiet, young, single mum who lives opposite Marin. She's doe-eyed, skinny as a stick, and clutching a large aluminium shovel.

"Use this!"

Jeni gives me her shovel then scrambles home, her arms folded tight. No dream, this. And here comes plucky Marin, swinging his own shovel. His red overalls are now white. He looks like some ace cricketer heading for the crease. Game on.

We pitch in and start digging. Perhaps the effort will warm me up? Seems not, this wind is too strong and far too cold. *God in heaven, what are we playing at? Fools, both of us.*

Beefy male neighbours appear at bright doorways along the lane, and three of them are soon working alongside us. We thrust and chuck, scoop and swing. Do it right and your snow sails over the fence. Do it wrong, snow blows in your face. Well, *my* face.

Angela peeps from the driver's window. "Shall I start the car?"

I shake my head. "No point, come and see."

She gets out for a better look. "Wow, still lots."

Our wheels are engulfed and our axles are asleep on a mattress of snow. Angela takes my arm. "You're shivering, get in the car."

I toss my shovel aside and clamber aboard. Hunched in my seat, I'm shaking like a wet dog. "Cold. Out there. So cold." The dashboard thermometer shows minus 12°C, but with that howling wind, it's minus brass monkeys. "Hat, please, Angela."

Angela rummages on the back seat. "Hat, yes, it should help."

I do love my black beret. A million Frenchmen can't be wrong. Although Frank Spencer was, often. Some mothers do 'ave 'em.

We sit watching our neighbours dig and dig and dig, side by side. They're frosted white. A line of snowmen making snowmen.

"Who's that with the ear flaps?" says Angela.

"Gheorghe, I think."

"He's pointing at us, should I start the car?"

"No, he's probably just wondering why I'm sitting in it."

Angela grabs my arm. "Stop, where are you're going?"

"Back out."

"But you'll–"

The blizzard snatches at my beret so I yank it down over my ears. My tweed jacket, usually so warm, offers scant protection from the wind. The snow is knee-deep and sticking to my jeans in clumps, as though I've stepped in a bucket of fresh meringue. We dig and chuck, dig and chuck. Faster, harder. Someone yells, *C'mon, lads!* But my gloveless hands throb, my feet are numb in these flimsy pumps, and I'm gasping for breath. *Twenty metres to go, to Marin's yard.* The snowmen thrust and swing their shovels, laughing and joking. Mother Winter poses little problem for these tough-nuts; she raised them, they grew up here. Not me. I'm exhausted. It's too cold. My heart thumps, as if I'm running up a sand dune. Time to stop. I'm done. No more. I'll just stand here. Rest. *I could lie down and sleep, even.*

"Domnul Mike!" Someone elbows me. Domnul Marin. His beard is a crust of ice, cracked by his grin. He's one happy Santa.

"What, Marin?"

"Dig, or you'll get cold! We're almost there!"

He points towards his house. Three little heads are at window, silhouetted against the light inside the house. His kids. Waiting for their *Tata*. I raise my shovel and ram it into snow. When the going gets tough, you don't sit down. That way, madness lies. And hyperthermia. *What was I thinking?* Dig or you'll die, more like.

It takes five of us forty minutes to clear the road to Marin's place. The snowmen help to push our car clear and Angela drives down into his yard. They slap high-fives and wobble away for a hit of hooch. *Want to come, Domnul Mike?* No, I want to go home.

Trekking up the ridge, carrying our bags, we pause at the top, stunned at what we see below us. The final stretch to our house is buried under a beautiful arc of purest white – a snowdrift fifty metres long that glistens in the dark. Waist-high in places, it froths gently along the crest, like an ocean wave. We plod along the lower edge, turning our heads away from the piercing wind. On a summer's day, we'd reach home in about thirty seconds. But this seems to take hours. I'm trembling with exhaustion, sucking air and exhaling wisps of white: in, out, in, out, in, out. *Breathe.*

"Well done, clearing that snow," says Angela, "but you must be cold."

"Cold. Yes. Feet. Hands."

Outside our door, Angela yanks hard on the icy cord to jangle the cowbell above. I stand and wait, shuddering and juddering, staring at icicles on the eaves; one is a metre long – a shining sword hanging over our heads. Damocles would approve: beware the perils of life, often unseen.

Eventually, the door creaks and little Uncle Nelu peeps out. He's wearing a flannel shirt, long johns, and a bobble hat that says *Ralph Lauren* across the front. His long, silver hair curls in horns, left and right, under his ear lobes. He looks like a designer elf.

"It's almost eight o'clock, I was in bed. What kept you?"

He crouches, fingers splayed, to brush a little snow from the mat in the hall, taking his time. I stumble up steps, clutching travel bags, desperate for refuge.

"Nelu, out the bloody way."

He moves aside and we lurch into the house. I drop the bags and squat near the log fire, staring into flames. My ears are roaring. My jaw hangs open. I feel strange. Focused but floaty. I'm here, but somewhere else. My body's in shock, or something. I've never, ever, felt this cold. Nelu pours shot glasses of *palinca*. I gulp mine, down in one. *Cheers.*

"So?" he says, rubbing tired eyes. It's a good question, and I'm buggered if I have the answer. All I know is, I've learned a few things the hard way. I've learned that a sunny day in the south can mean a blizzard up north. I've learned to pack boots and a shovel in the car, come November. I've also learned something about how it might feel to freeze to death. *You just go to sleep.*

Tango's Foxtrot

They call him Tango. A handsome man in his early forties, he is broad of shoulder, bandy of leg, and the best dancer by far in these hills. On special occasions, such as New Year's Eve, Tango sports a gold ring on every finger and twirls the life out of his pretty little wife, on the floor of the village hall, with his billowing white smock unbuttoned to expose his hairless, bronzed chest. The life and soul of any party. Handsome, too.

The rest of the year, Tango herds his sheep, milks his cows, and brews his hooch. He's got four kids, all baptised, and a guest house painted pink. Ten bedrooms and plenty of clients, rain or shine. Most of Tango's neighbours will tell you straight. *Tango? He's an arsehole. Lowest of the low.* Perhaps they're envious.

We spot Tango quite frequently when we're out walking our dogs. He'll be on his hill, in his yard, or bumping along a potholed lane in his dusty pick-up. We'll get a wave, a twinkly smile, and sometimes an invitation yelled through cupped hands. *Come to mine, glass of wine!* Sometimes, we accept and soon find ourselves perched on tiny wooden stools in a cramped and cluttered kitchen that serves also as a lounge, bedroom, and barn. Anything goes and lots of things come, including a hen. We rather enjoy our occasional visits, as do the various kids and kittens who wobble at our feet. On warm days, Tango's wife serves us glasses of sweet rosé. On cold days, we get little cups of mulled wine. A big plastic Rolex, one metre in length, hangs vertically on the wall and stopped long ago.

Tango's eighty-year-old mother, however, is going strong. Doamna Letiția wears two headscarves, several layers of clothing, hand-knitted woollen socks – two on each foot – and a stout leather belt. If you need a jumble sale, look no further. Miki the hen roosts in her lap, neck feathers shimmering like a rainbow as she stares at us, black eyes beady: *Who the cluck?*

Doamna Letiția could yap for Romania. *Yap yap.* She tells us tales from the old days, some of which make our tails curl.

"Thirteen abortions, I've had!" Doamna Letiția sounds rather proud, caressing her Miki. "Did some myself. You soak ten razor blades in wine, until they melt, then drink the wine."

Tango's eldest daughter sits and listens. Maria is twelve going on twenty, and very pretty. Break some hearts, she will. Angela seems reluctant to pursue the grim discussion, but it intrigues me. Letiția's potion sounds like part of some medieval spell.

"Then what, Doamna?"

"Then, no more baby." Letiția shrugs, adjusting the knots of headscarves, under her chin. *That's life.*

Tango's craggy-faced father, Domnul Octavian straddles a little wooden stool nearby, listening in silence; his overalls are baggy, his clogs are rubber, and his conical felt hat belongs in a circus. He gazes at his wife and nods his head, as if bemused by the mysteries of making babies. He turns away to poke a steel rod into the wood-burning cavity of the old iron *sobă*. A cat dozes on the hotplate, which can't be very hot. Octavian looks at the cat, then into the *sobă*. He's a gimlet-eyed man of few words, but they usually count.

"Hey, fire's gone out!"

His announcement functions like a cue in a stage play: a side door swings open and Tango waddles into the room, carrying three fat logs. He shakes our hands, firmly.

"Domnul Mike! Doamna Angela!"

He seems to have forgotten that he invited us, just fifteen minutes ago. But that's ok because Tango doesn't forget when your glass needs a refill, like now.

Midwinter brings water problems. The supply from our communal spring up a nearby hill seems to have stopped. *Frozen pipe? Bust pump?* We don't know, but a dozen homes are affected at this end of the village, including ours. We're all without water – *fără apă* – for several hours each day. It's not the first time and won't be the last. The odd thing is, water returns when we least expect. *How come?*

One afternoon, we mention it to Tango while he's unloading supplies from the back of his little truck – sacks of potatoes, butane gas bottles, and several crates of beer to sell to clients at his guest house. He's expecting quite a few people this weekend and will turn a pretty profit, no doubt. I reckon Tango's doing well financially, despite his worn-out clothes, higgledy-piggledy little home, and cranking old car.

Good for him. Diversification, and all that? Maybe this is why he's always smiling. Maybe this is why so many locals dislike him. Perhaps they wish they had more clients. Perhaps they would get some, if they spruced up their own guest rooms and posted some snaps online.

Angela talks and Tango looks very concerned as he lurches to-and-fro, lugging his supplies. He takes a break and clicks his teeth at our dogs. They jostle around him, sniffing his hands, dusty pants, and old boots. He fondles their ears.

"Still no water, you say, Doamna Angela? That's bad. That's terrible. You and Domnul Mike need your own spring, like we've got."

His bright-eyed wife Tamara emerges from the guest house, wearing rubber gloves and carrying a mop and bucket. "Hi, guys! Doamna Angela, how's our website coming?"

"I'm almost done. But, it's not really a website."

"Oh, I thought you said you'd make us one?"

"No, you asked for a page on Airbnb, at least, as far as I remember?" Angela glances at me. *Website?* I shrug.

Tamara laughs. "Whatever. How's life with you?"

We tell her we have no water. She pouts and offers her condolences, but, if we'll excuse her, she has work to do and must refill her bucket. Tango grabs another crate of beer. "Me too, work work. Bye, guys. Come for a glass, sometime. Miki misses you."

On Christmas Day, *Moș Crăciun* brings us gifts – a silk scarf for Angela and woollen socks for me – but no water. We consult a neighbouring shepherd as he passes our house. Domnul Abel is trying to cajole six fluffy sheep up the lane, but they keep stopping to nuzzle for shoots of grass in the snow. Good luck with that.

"Is the main pipe frozen, Abel?" says Angela.

He grins, half-sloshed, and tells us *no*, the communal pipe is too deep underground to freeze.

"Our problem lies elsewhere, Doamna." He winks at us, taps his beaky nose, and walks on, swinging a stick. It's all a bit of a puzzle, at least for us. Domnul Abel is an enigma wrapped in a jumper wrapped in a tatty old coat.

But rumours travel fast between these snow-capped mountains, and you can't keep a good one down. Eventually, our questions prompt an intriguing answer from the jolly widow a few cottages along. Doamna Dana brings us milk, warm as a cow shed. We sit at our kitchen table. I serve tea and Angela offers thick slices of home-made banana cake. Doamna Dana has never tasted any, until now. It blows her mind and loosens her tongue.

"Doamna Angela, guess why we get no water down here? It's that lot, up there. They let their standpipes run all night so water won't freeze and their livestock can drink it next day. It's them standpipes what empty the communal tanks. Just think how many standpipes are running, all night? It's that lot."

"Which *lot?*" says Angela.

Dana glances around. Perhaps she thinks our house is bugged. She grew up under Communist spooks, after all. She leans closer. "It's my neighbour, for a start, that Ionescu is a sly one."

"Really? Perhaps I'll ask him."

Angela phones Domnul Ionescu and puts the call on speaker, so we can hear. Dana sits bug eyed, munching.

Domnul Ionescu sounds guarded, at first, but soon spills his beans. "Very well. I won't lie to you, Doamna Angela. Yes, I do let my standpipe run all night. May I ask who told you?"

We glance at Dana. She shakes her head, and Angela says, "Never mind who told me, Domnul Ionescu, but, please, stop your standpipe at night? You're emptying the communal tanks and twelve families farther down the lane have no water. Please stop?"

"Fine, I'll stop. But your problem won't."

"How do you mean?"

"Never mind, *how do I mean.*" The line clicks and he's gone.

Dana reaches for more cake. "Told you so. And I want this recipe in time for New Year."

The cowbell above our front door jangles next morning, and we find half a dozen grim-faced local men gathered in the lane. Our diminutive, dark-eyed neighbour Titus seems to be in charge, flanked by his skinny brother Iacob and beefy, moonfaced Domnul Horia. Titus wears a tracksuit, no hat, and no gloves. It's only minus 9°C, after all. He peeps through our slatted gate.

"We're going to Tango's place. Please join us, Doamna Angela? For ten minutes, is all."

"For what," says Angela, "mulled wine?"

"Not today. Have you got water, yet?"

"We had some last night, briefly, but not now."

"Same here, and we think we know why. It's not just Domnul Ionescu's fault. He told me all about your phone call, but there's more to this. So, please come?"

"If you insist, although, why me? I can't fix a broken pump."

"But you run our monthly payments book, Doamna, so we think you should see for yourself, in case we're right."

"Right about what?"

"You'll see. We've had a tip-off."

I speak over Angela's shoulder. "Frozen pipe, is it, Titus?"

He gives me a wink. "Come and find out, Domnul Mike."

What we find, on Tango's snowy sloping field, is a classic example of *șmecherie*. Foul play, sneakiness, wily scheming, double-dealing, slyness, you name it. A rascal practises *șmecheria*, because he or she is *șmecher*. I love how that sounds: 'sh-meh-ka'.

Tango spots our gang on his land and plods through snow, smiling at us. "Guys, what's up?" Perhaps he doesn't know.

Titus is flat on his tummy in the snow, craning his neck into a concrete pit, thirty centimetres square. He's got a flashlight and bad news. "Just as we thought." He extracts his head from the pit, and rises to his feet, breathing hard. "Tango, you scumbag."

"Me?"

"You conniving piece of shit."

Tango wags a stubby finger. "Titus, you'd better stop–"

"No, Tango, you'd better shut up. Twelve families have been without water over Christmas, because you cut us off. Diverted our supply to your guest house, didn't you?"

"Me? I don't know anything about–"

"Really? So, who turned off this fucking tap on your land?"

"You did. Just now. I saw you reaching in."

"What? I just turned it *on*, you toad! And tomorrow, I'll bring a wrench and remove that damned tap for good. You did this last year too, didn't you, I bet? Well, now we caught you. Out of my way, I don't want to fight. C'mon, folks, we're all done here."

Tango stands aside, looking baffled. Or trying his best.

"Guys! I don't need water from the communal spring! I have my own and you know it!"

We trudge past him, single-file. Nobody replies, except Titus.

"Yes, Tango, we know about your spring. Full of fish and frogs and cow shit. It's a puddle of piss, your spring. That's why you diverted ours, you șmecher."

Tango's elderly father Domnul Octavian strides from their barn, wearing checked pants, his conical felt hat, and a waistcoat with big yellow buttons. He looks like a clown, but he's not smiling.

"Titus, you fucking midget, get off our land!"

Next morning, our group reconvenes. Ten of us, including Angela and me. Titus is carrying a big black wrench.

"For that blasted tap. Let's go!"

His brother Iacob has brought a bulging canvas tool bag, just in case. We trudge up the lane towards Tango's land. There are few words spoken along the way. Our actions will speak for us.

Tango is waiting when we arrive. He's leaning against a stack of silver birch branches, the sort the farmers give to their sheep to nibble. Seems there's something in the bark that prevents liver worm. How anyone discovered it, I've no idea, but that's folklore for you – people sharing their ideas and wisdom. Today, there's only animosity. Tango has a surly expression, hands tucked in his pockets. Keeping a safe distance, Titus stops and points with the wrench towards the concrete pit, off to one side, ten metres away.

"I've come to remove your tap. Don't try and stop me."

Tango grabs a stout birch branch from his stack, trots bandy-legged down the slope and whacks Titus over the head. Titus reels under the glancing blow, swinging his wrench at Tango, who turns and runs towards a barn. He slips through the side door and disappears into the darkness. Sheepdogs on chains snap and snarl as Titus races after him, wrench raised.

Angela yells, "Titus, stop! You'll kill him and go to prison!"

Titus turns and walks back to us, rubbing his head. "Bastard got me." He strides on, to the concrete pit. "Iacob, tool bag."

Tango's father Domnul Octavian steps from behind a huge haystack, waving a rusty pitchfork.

"Titus, I warned you, get off our fucking land!"

I'm closest and block his progress down the slope, my arms out like aeroplane wings.

"Domnul Octavian, no!"

We shimmy left and right. He spits and curses, looking straight through me, frothing at the mouth like some deranged horse. Some of the other fellows scurry to my side and Domnul Octavian backs off, jabbing his pitchfork at the overcast sky. *Titus, you fucking midget!*

Titus is too busy to care. He pulls the warped wooden lid off the concrete pit, slithers onto his tummy, and sticks his head inside. Iacob squats nearby, passing him a spanner from the bag.

Angela phones the police, just in case. *We've got trouble in Culmea.* They promise to come, maybe, but not soon. Because the roads are bad. And they don't know the exact address. Angela pleads, tells them we're at Tango's place, there's been a fight, it could start again. Tango's twelve-year-old daughter Maria turns up, all ears. Her pretty brown eyes scan the scene. She joins her grandfather, presumably for an update. He's clutching his rusty pitchfork, muttering and scowling, his conical hat askew.

Titus is still leaning into the pit twenty minutes later, because removing the water tap is proving harder than expected. Some of the other fellows lean in to offer advice. Iacob rummages for tools.

This one, Titus? Or this?

The cops turn up, eventually. They're clean-shaven, quietly spoken, and wear Russian-style hats of synthetic blue fur with shiny badges. They want to talk to Angela. She explains what happened and why Titus has two injuries – a gash on his scalp and a graze on his temple. The cops seem almost indifferent.

The elusive Tango emerges from his refuge, all smiles and carrying a long, rusty spanner. He greets the cops warmly but seems preoccupied – places to go and things to do.

"Morning, Officers! Just going to help my friend Titus. Back in a minute!"

The cops look at Angela, as if to say, *He's the bad guy?* Angela looks at me, baffled. I follow Tango down the slope.

He squats near the pit, and says, in a loud voice for all to hear, "Hey, Titus, my friend, try this tool I brought. Works well."

Titus doesn't even bother to look up. "Fuck you, Tango."

Tango edges closer, speaking in a low voice. "Oh, come now, don't be upset, Titus, and please don't tell the cops what happened. Maybe you and I will drink some wine later, eh?"

"I've got wine at home. Leave me alone, I'm busy."

Tango walks back up the slope and bums a cigarette from one of the cops. *Thank you, Officer.* It's a clever, even ingratiating move, seeing as he never smokes. He puffs away, listening to Angela's version of events. After a few moments, he cuts in.

"No, Doamna Angela, you're mistaken. Titus attacked *me*, with that large and dangerous wrench. I acted in self-defence."

Angela's jaw sags. "Are you serious?"

"Yes, he was trespassing. He threatened me."

"You clobbered him with a branch, unprovoked."

"After he raised his wrench to hit me. I acted in self-defence."

"And what about Domnul Octavian bringing his pitchfork? Was that for *self-defence,* too?"

"Actually," says pretty young Maria, "Grandpa was only using a pitchfork to feed dry grass to our sheep. That's all." She smiles at the policemen. *It's true.*

I know that smile; see it every week when she attends my ukulele class. Quick learner, this one.

131

"Maria," says Angela, "I think you should go home and enjoy your childhood while you can, don't you?"

Maria doesn't. She stays and watches to listen and learn.

The biggest cop turns to Tango. "Well, technically speaking, sir, Domnul Titus was not actually trespassing on your land."

"How do you work that out?" Tango edges closer, all matey, sucking and blowing smoke. He doesn't inhale; it's just for show.

There's something else, come to think of it: when Tango dances with his wife at the village hall, he doesn't actually *tango.* He just careens around the room, whooping and whistling, clicking his fingers and stamping his feet, until everyone stands back, out of his way, and applauds. On and on he goes, spinning and spinning, until you feel nauseous just watching.

Back in Five

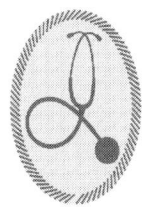

Angela doesn't want lunch. Not even a cup of tea. She just wants to lie on the sofa and rest awhile in her fleecy pyjamas, and considerable discomfort. "Hardly slept last night," she says, with a grimace. She stretches and twists, groaning gently.

I perch on the edge of the sofa. "Is the pain in your back?"

"Not in my back. Just… somewhere inside. It's not nice."

At times like this, I wish our remote village had a doctor, even a nurse. But the nearest one is seven kilometres down a winding road through the forest. How many times have Angela and I discussed the uncertainty of our future, when we'll be old and infirm with nobody to look after us, and no medics nearby?

I stand at our big windows, wondering what to do. A snow-covered valley sprawls below the house and a ridge of steep mountains soar in the distance like a tsunami of rock and ice. Our horizon is a sheer cliff of rock, a thousand metres high. Sometimes it seems like a wall, blocking us in. Perhaps our future is now.

"Should we drive to the hospital in Dumbrăvița, Angela?"

"Maybe." She places the back of her wrist on her eyes.

"Is the pain worse than it was yesterday?"

"Hard to tell, I'm tired. It's the same but different, somehow."

"Sharper, duller, bigger? Does it ache or throb?"

"The pain is the same but seems to have moved."

This sounds worryingly familiar. "The pain has *moved*?"

Angela traces a finger across her tummy. "From here to here."

"That's not good. You might need surgery."

"Surgery?" She gives me a troubled look. "For what?"

"Appendicitis. The pain moves from left to right, I think."

"How do you know?"

"It happened to me. They took it out." I reach for Angela's hand; it feels clammy and hot. "Get up, madam. We're going to Brașov."

"*Brașov?* You said Dumbrăvița. Why Brașov?"

"Because if this is appendicitis, time is crucial."

"It will take us ninety minutes to get to Brașov."

"Probably longer in this snow. Sit up, time to get dressed."

"Dumbrăvița is only forty minutes away."

"Better safe than sorry. I doubt they can operate in Dumbrăvița."

"But they'll know what's wrong, Mike, and it's a lot closer."

"If this is appendicitis and we delay, there's a good chance you'll get peritonitis."

"What's that?"

"Your appendix bursts, then you've got no chance. So?"

She slides off the sofa, wincing. "Let's go to Brașov." The white cat at her feet mews in protest. Angela hobbles up the stairs, groaning all the way and I help her, one step at a time, offering crucial words of comfort.

"You can borrow my teddy bear."

The road out of our village is a seeping, weeping mess of slush and snow – the melting remains of a blizzard that lasted some five days, and the reason we've not driven anywhere for the past three or four weeks. It was the same last winter – we were snowbound for a month, blasted by bone-chilling winds and temperatures of minus 20°C. Ironic, really, considering how so many summer tourists tell us we live in paradise.

The car slithers and slides, its wheels grinding in vain for traction. "How are you feeling, Angela?"

"Not great. Drive slowly, Mike."

My watch says 14.45. Ahead of us lie seven kilometres of steep hairpin bends through dense forest. In this weather, we're unlikely to meet any other cars, trucks, or hikers. That's the good news. The bad news is, once we reach the main road, we've got another forty kilometres to the hospital.

A wretched-looking, snow-covered dog watches in silence, as we growl past the last house in the village. The dog is chained to a post. No kennel, no bark, no fun. We drive on, down into the valley of darkness, through which we will pass as pronto as possible, ice and snow permitting.

"Did you remember to close the garage door?" says Angela, and I nod, hoping I'm right.

The middle-aged receptionist at the hospital wears a woollen bonnet, a green pinafore, and an encouraging smile. She tells us we must put on protective plastic bootees and sells us two pairs from a little box in her glass-walled kiosk. They're like shower caps, bright blue, with elastic edges for a close fit. *Nice.*

Appropriately dressed, we pass through various doors and search for helpful signs, but there are none. A whey-faced orderly asks us what we want. He's wearing red overalls and a faux-fur hat. A laminated badge dangles from a lanyard around his neck, showing his photo. He's not smiling in that either.

Clutching her tummy, Angela asks for the emergency clinic. The orderly points a nicotine-stained finger.

"Upstairs. Left, right, then diagonal."

"Thanks, will there be signs?"

"Signs for what?"

"For the emergency clinic, when I get upstairs?"

"We don't have signs. But it's easy to find and you'll know when you're there. "

"How will I know?"

"Because there'll be a big queue. You can't miss it." Our advisor wanders off.

We plod upstairs. As it turns out, he was wrong about easy directions, but right about the queue, which consists of some thirty morose-looking souls leaning against the walls or slumped on wooden benches in a narrow corridor that smells of cabbage. They gawp into space or poke at the dressings on their bashed head, sprained arm, squashed foot.

Half-open doors reveal rooms of various sizes containing patients, nurses, doctors, and more orderlies. In one room, a large, disorderly gentleman sports a neck brace of sturdy, grey plastic. He's lurching in circles and looks troubled. Heading our way, now, towards the corridor.

"Mama, enough! I'm going home!" He whines, like a jittery child, at an elderly woman in a paisley headscarf.

She strides after him. "Easy, now, they won't hurt you." She reaches out, tries to shepherd her belligerent son towards a young female medic in a white tunic and white clogs.

"No, Mama! I want to go home!" The son veers away, increasingly distressed. He lumbers past us and into the corridor, wide-eyed. He scans the walls, presumably for an exit sign.

His mother follows, trying again to coax him back. He shoves her aside like a bear swatting a troublesome terrier. She yelps a curse, pleading for help. Nobody intervenes. Everyone watches. We retreat to sit on a bench, out of harm's way, and the slanging match continues. *No security staff?*

A short and stocky, bald-headed orderly in red overalls appears. He saunters towards the big, whingeing man. The orderly is chewing gum, hands tucked in his pockets. "Wanna go home, huh?"

"Yes, I've had enough." The big man sniffles, dabbing his wrist at weepy eyes.

The orderly unclips the neck brace. The big man squirms. "No, wait, what are you doing?"

The orderly walks away, waving the brace. "Just making sure you don't take this."

The big man stares at his mother, who stares back at him and shakes her head. *You bad boy.*

After a short wait, it's Angela's turn to see a doctor, up the corridor. I follow her into a small room

137

containing a gurney, desk, chairs, cupboards, and a sink. Charts and posters line the walls; most advertise medication, but one shows the chambers inside a human heart. It's quite fascinating to see, up close like this, where all your love, and doubt, and stress goes: in and out, round and about.

The doctor is a skinny, middle-aged fellow with a sharp face and a blotchy complexion. His hair is dyed an unlikely shade of black and coiled in an Elvis quiff. He's quite good-looking for his age, and, in a perfect world, he'd be wearing a black leather jacket, drainpipe jeans, and brothel creepers. Instead, in this one, he's slumped inside an acrylic sweater, baggy corduroy pants, and brown sandals. He makes no eye contact and seems reluctant to acknowledge our presence. So much for bedside manner. He gazes at his PC and murmurs, "Yes?"

Angela explains her symptoms. The doctor listens, still eyeing his screen. He's probably heard it all before, except perhaps her final line.

"Which is why my husband is worried I might have appendicitis," says Angela.

The doctor averts his gaze to smile at her, then at me. *You reckon?* He drums three fingers on his sweater, then stands up. To prove us wrong, I hope. He summons Angela to the gurney and points at a chair for me: *Sit.* I do as I am told, and if I had a tail, I'd wag it.

The doctor takes Angela's blood pressure, peering at the readout. "Bit high, Doamna."

"Perhaps I'm a bit nervous?" says Angela. The doctor repeats the test, and this time the results are a bit lower. He returns to his desk, scribbles on a green form, and gives it to her. He points to the door. "Wait in the corridor. Someone else will see you soon."

So far, so good, but his handwriting could be Egyptian hieroglyphics for all the sense it makes. Angela reads it and glances at me. She looks puzzled, as she folds the form in half.

"Thank you, Doctor, but, any idea what's causing my pain?"

He stares at his PC, and sighs. "Not appendicitis."

We wait in the corridor, on a bench with a slatted wooden seat. Angela seems less stressed than earlier. She leans towards me. "That was pretty quick. I thought it would take a lot longer."

I can only agree. It's a while since we've needed a hospital, but we've heard some ominous tales in the meantime, from relatives and friends, about interminable delays and dodgy diagnoses. And that's just in the UK, where some Brits reckon the National Health Service is falling apart, although others remain stoically proud of it. *How will Angela's case be handled, here in regional Romania?* We watch for a helpful medic or nurse, but none comes. Oh, well.

I don't mind waiting as long as I've got something to read. I root in my knapsack and pull out a recent copy of *The New Yorker*. Scanning the table of contents, I spot a long story about healthcare in the Himalayas. How appropriate. The photos of Nepal are breathtaking and the text profiles a brave, female doctor who delivers medicine, riding for many weeks on a bareback mule.

An hour and a half later, I know how she feels. My bum is numb.

Nurses glide past us clutching documents, syringes, and small white cartons. Gurneys trundle by – one carries a toothless crone with a plastic tube coming from her arm; one bears a young man whose bloodied head is wrapped in a bandage. The other patients sag against the walls, snooze on benches, or amble up and down, waiting for their names to be announced on the intercom. We've heard several names, but not *Angela Nicoară*. She's still watching and waiting, perched on the edge of our bench, for the elusive somebody who was supposed to help. So far, so confusing.

Angela shows me her watch. "It's seven o'clock. That doctor said *soon*."

"Maybe they announced your name, but you missed it?"

"No, I've been listening. I don't think they even know I'm here."

"Perhaps you're supposed to go and give them the document he filled in?"

"He told me to wait in the corridor. He didn't say I had to give this green form in."

"Yes, but look around: you're the only person holding one."

Angela looks around. "True. How come?"

"Ask this nurse in the squeaky shoes. Show her your form."

"I will, this pain is getting worse."

Angela stands up, clutching her lower back and waving her green form. The pretty young nurse pauses to read it and looks baffled. "Hmm, I see. And you arrived *when*, did you say?"

"Five-fifteen. The doctor saw me at five-thirty. He said someone would see me soon. My back hurts, it's getting worse."

The nurse checks her chunky yellow Swatch. "It's after seven o'clock. You've been waiting an hour and a half? That's too long."

"Please, could you give my form to someone inside?" says Angela, gesturing towards the treatment rooms.

"Yes, I'll take your form and give it to someone inside."

"Should I wait here?"

"Yes, you should wait here."

"And someone will call me, on the intercom?"

"Yes, someone will call you on the intercom."

The nurse walks away, holding the form. She's been helpful, I suppose, but those robotic answers hardly inspire me. What if Angela had asked, *Is the earth flat?* Never mind, at least things are moving, and so is the nurse. Her shoes squeak as she pads away, along the corridor. She squeezes past a gurney, sidesteps a wandering child, and slips through a trio of worried-looking teenagers dressed in stonewashed jeans and training shoes.

"I just noticed something else, Angela."

"What?"

"We're the only people wearing blue plastic bootees."

"You're right, so much for germs."

"I'm going to take mine off. My feet are getting hot."

Half an hour later, bootee-less, we're still waiting. Nobody comes, nobody asks. *Good job it's not appendicitis.*

On the bench opposite ours, a hollow-cheeked girl asks the man alongside her if she might borrow his phone because she needs to make a call, but is out of credit. She's also out of luck because he refuses and looks a bit grumpy about being asked, dipping his chin into the neck of his sweater, as if to prevent further inquiries.

The girl glances around, kicking her heels. Lime-green jeans cling to her emaciated legs, and her pale grey eyes are set wide in a pinched face. It's hard to tell how old she is, given her frail build and wan complexion; *sixteen or twenty-six?* Something of the street kid about her, too – a savvy tough-nut, perhaps. But she looks a bit lost in this world of worried grown-ups.

Angela leans forward and offers the girl her iPhone.

"Excuse me, Domnișoară? You can use mine."

The girl seems surprised and grateful. "Wow, thanks a lot, Doamna. Nice phone, but could you dial the number for me?"

"Sure, read it out." Angela waits, finger poised.

The girl holds up her own phone. "This number, Doamna."

Angela peers at the screen. "Sorry, forgot my glasses. Could you just tell me?"

The girl crosses the corridor to sit on our bench, wiggling between us like a pup who just got adopted.

"Thing is, Doamna, I don't have much school. I don't know numbers and words, see."

"Oh, well, let's try again, shall we?"

Angela takes the girl's battered Nokia and asks me to tell her the number on the screen. I read it aloud, she thumbs the number into her screen and hands the iPhone to the girl, who gets up and wanders off, chatting away. Angela sits back, with a contended sigh. *Nice to help.* Then the penny drops, and she says, "Mike, that girl's got my iPhone. I hope it wasn't a scam."

"Probably not, she's coming back."

The girl walks towards us, but then turns around and walks away again, still chatting on the phone. She seems in no hurry.

"How many units you got, Angela?"

"Plenty, Mike, and it was a local number, so no problem."

Eventually, the girl returns, and gives the iPhone back to Angela, all smiles. "Thanks a lot, Doamna. At least now they know where I am and they won't worry."

She sits on a different bench, keeping her distance from the grumpy man who wouldn't help. She looks at a poster on the wall, but not for long. Life must be difficult as an illiterate youngster and I doubt it will get easier as she grows older.

I open my magazine and continue reading – a simple and rewarding activity that I take for granted, perhaps. I try to see the text through the eyes of someone who cannot read, but it's impossible because every word triggers a response. A more accurate test would be for me to try and read Chinese, with its strange doodles. *That's how it must feel, to be that girl.* I watch her fiddling with her shoelaces. She takes her time to untie and tie them, poking out the tip of her tongue.

I flip a page in my magazine. The next article is about rising sea levels, and scientists who reckon a sudden flooding of the Black Sea, about seven thousand years ago, may have inspired the story of the deluge in the book of Genesis. As for modern times, Greenland has enough ice to raise global sea levels by twenty feet, and guess what, it's melting. Given how long we might have to wait in this hospital, perhaps we should have kept our plastic bootees.

"Whatever happened to that nurse with my form?" says Angela, rubbing her back. She's no hypochondriac but clearly in distress.

Perhaps it's time to play our trump card. I'm a bit reluctant to do so since it seems unfair on the other patients, but we've been waiting longer than most of them, and I've lived abroad long enough to know that when all else fails, just being a foreigner can open the doors that remain inexplicably closed to locals.

I lean closer to my wife. "Time for the Baffled Brit?"

Angela nods. "Off you go, but speak English not Romanian."

I walk up the corridor and through a doorway to where the action is or rather isn't. The room is big and spacious, with a few beds – some unoccupied – and about twenty staff including doctors, nurses, clerks, and orderlies. Most of them seem busy being busy. They stand and chat, or sit and gaze earnestly at computer screens. Three women are gathered at a small, square table; one scribbles in a ledger, the others sit back and sip drinks from plastic beakers. One fellow taps a sheaf of A4 documents on his desk to align them along the bottom edge. Obviously, such things matter in an emergency unit. The atmosphere feels relaxed rather than business-like; I detect no sense of urgency and see no flapping white coat tails or worried brows. A passing nurse pauses to ask me what I want. I try my best to appear bemused, which is easy in the circumstances.

"Thank you, Nurse, do you speak English?"

"A little bit, why?"

The nurse folds her arms and cocks her head, as I explain.

"I'm sorry to intrude, since you're all so busy, but my wife is in considerable pain. We've been waiting out there, in the corridor, for two hours. One of your colleagues took her form and said–"

The nurse leans sideways to look towards the doorway behind me. "Your wife's been waiting in the corridor for two hours?"

"Correct, and as I said, one of–"

"Come this way, please."

The nurse leads me to a long table, upon which, side by side, sit several green forms. She points at them.

"Show me, which form?"

I scan the names on the forms. "This one, this is her form."

The nurse reads it and rolls her eyes. "Bring your wife, now. Then you wait in the corridor, please."

I walk back to the corridor and beckon Angela, who shuffles towards me, hunched in pain. Some of the other patients catch my eye and seem to have suspicious minds, like Dr Elvis. I know how they feel. *But what if he was wrong in the first place?*

At eight o'clock, half an hour after she went into the big room, Angela emerges, walking baby steps. She's holding a plastic bottle of liquid, from which a transparent plastic tube snakes into her right arm, secured by a beige dressing. She looks pale and tired.

"Hi, Mike. They gave me an ECG, took a blood sample, and put me on this drip for the pain."

"Is it helping?"

"Yes, a lot. Now I'm going for an echograph."

"I thought you just had one?"

"That was ECG, electrocardiograph, electrodes. Echograph's different, it uses ultrasound instead."

"Electrodes, eh, so did you confess?"

"Yes, told them everything. They reckon it's a good job we came. So, thanks for bringing me."

"My pleasure. See you in, oh, three hours?"

In fact, Angela returns in ten minutes, looking disgruntled. "Quickest echograph ever, that was."

I close my magazine. "How do you mean?"

"Well, in my experience, an echograph usually takes ages. They go back and forth, left and right, up and down with that scanner thing, the handset. But here, the nurse just ran it once across my chest like she was swiping a visa card, then she says, *You're done*."

"At least you didn't have to wait. Now what?"

"I have to wait."

"Excellent notion."

"And I forgot my glasses. What are you reading?"

"*New Yorker*. Did you know, sea levels could rise between ten and thirty feet, by 2100? It's a good job we live in the mountains."

"Good job we won't be alive."

"Right, I forgot about that. How's the back?"

"Better, this drip is magic. I feel ready to go home."

A passing orderly gives Angela a small plastic tube with a yellow cap and says, "Not so fast, Doamna. Urine test, remember?"

When she gets back from the loo, Angela leads me up the corridor. "Nurse said I have to go to a different place and wait."

We pass through double doors, into a room containing several grimacing grannies and a middle-aged man whose shirt is unbuttoned to the waist. His belly resembles a balloon that could pop, any minute. A medic in a white coat straps a black band on the man's arm and says, "Christ Almighty, are you fat or what?"

The man shrugs and his tummy wobbles. "I am a bit, yes."

"A *bit*? What do you eat for breakfast, half a pig?"

"Can't afford meat, me. Just coffee, that's all I have."

"My arse. No one gets this fat on coffee. How much sugar in your coffee, Big Guy?"

"Me? One spoon."

"One kilo, more like. You'll have a heart attack, one day."

"I already did. That's why I came."

"Oh, I get it. Came to the hospital so we can fix you, Fatso? What a joke. Anyway, shut up, while I check your blood pressure."

Some of the grannies watch with baleful expressions. One of them seems more interested in a mucky bandage on her withered leg. She mutters at it, then waits as if expecting a reply. The medic finishes the test and waddles out; Slim Jim he ain't.

The room has a gurney for Angela to lie on, and a chair for me. Its leatherette seat slopes badly and the backrest seems to have been designed to torture any occupant. Nevertheless, I sit in it, grateful we have access to this hospital, even if it is far away from our home and moves slower than a glacier in Greenland.

Angela looks bored, lying on her gurney. I offer my magazine and point to a cartoon showing a medieval army marching away from a distant fort. The army's leader, sitting upfront on a horse, asks a colleague: *Did we remember to close the drawbridge?*

Angela grins. "Just like us, with the garage. Did you close it?"

"Think so. How's your back?"

"Miles better, thanks. I'm starting to wonder why I'm here."

"You'll remember when the painkiller runs out."

"Probably. I feel a bit tired. Perhaps it's the drip."

"Who are we waiting for, apart from Godot?"

"My results. I'm definitely feeling a bit woozy, you know."

"What happens if you fail all their tests?"

"Probably keep me in. Actually, I think I'll have a little nap."

"Or even a big one."

"Hush."

Angela settles down for a sleep. The fat man across the room pokes at his phone and speaks in a loud voice.

"It's me, I'm OK. But the staff are quite rude about my weight." He listens, shakes his head, and says into the phone, "Great, thanks, so it's *my* fault?"

Another two hours pass. Nurses come and go. The granny with the bad leg whinges and wheezes, unbuttons and buttons her tatty cardigan, rearranges her headscarf, and talks to her bandage.

Angela seems refreshed after her sleep and chats with a dark-skinned, silver-haired woman wearing a yellow top, gold necklace, and a bright, paisley-patterned skirt, who is propped on the next gurney. Her appearance suggests she's Roma. Her shoes are underneath the gurney, side by side, and their straps appear to have been partly chewed by a dog. She covers her holed socks with her coat, either for warmth or from shame. She glances left and right.

"Blimmin' nurses. Don't tell you anything. I arrived at noon. Noon!"

"Did someone bring you?" Angela asks.

"No, I live alone. Don't see much of my son, these days."

"Have you phoned him, at least?"

"We don't speak. But he's doing *very* well. Nice house, big car. You'd never think he was related to someone like me." Her gracious smile is tinged with regret and I look away, engulfed by a surge of sadness. What a pitiful thing for a mother to say.

The fat man drones into his phone, on and on. He ends one loud chat and dials a number to start another one. *Chain-caller, addicted, with a thousand minutes of credit?* I flip forward to the next article in my magazine. This place does your head in.

I'm reading – or trying to read – about an African American comedienne named Leslie Jones, who struggled for twenty-five years against racism and sexism among managers and booking agencies. But now she's a star and wants us to remember: *black women have the hardest gig in showbiz*. And she should know.

"Angela Nicoară?" A nurse enters the room, hands on hips.

"Yes, that's me." Angela raises a finger.

The nurse removes the drip from Angela's arm. "You can go."

"Oh, great, thanks – but do you have the results?"
"Results?"
"Of my blood test, urine test, ECG, and echograph?"

"No idea." The nurse coils the tube. "I'll ask, you wait here."

She leaves the room.

We're still waiting here half an hour later. Angela slides off the gurney says, "Great, just great. I'll go and find out for myself."

We walk into the corridor of lost souls. We're halfway up it, peeping left and right into various rooms, in search of the previous nurse, when a different one appears with a sheaf of documents.

"Angela Nicoară? I was just coming to find you." She leads us back into the big room full of doctors and points to a bed. "Wait."

Angela lies down on the bed. After a few minutes, a young male doctor ambles up, hands in his pockets. He has ginger hair and keen brown eyes. "Hi, there! So, what's wrong with you?"

Angela tells him what she's already told half a dozen of his colleagues over the last six hours. He listens carefully, then pokes her gently in the tummy. "But you're feeling better now, right?"

"Yes, Doctor, because they put me on a drip."

"I see. Well, wait here, while I check. Back in five."

He walks away and doesn't return. Fifteen minutes later, a different doctor turns up, points to Angela, and says to a passing nurse. "So, what's up with this lady?"

The nurse shrugs. "No problem, I think she's leaving soon."

They walk away, presumably to attend to someone who isn't.

"Incredible," says Angela, rising from the bed. We walk to a table where three patients are sitting chatting to an older doctor, but he's too busy to notice us. We stand around wondering what to do. I'm starting to feel as if I live in a painting by Salvador Dali, where the clocks are melting.

A male voice booms from behind green curtains. "Is *anyone* helping in this place? I've waited too long. If nobody helps, I'll…"

The voice fades to silence. The green curtains are yanked back to reveal a man wearing only shorts and socks. He wanders the room, presumably looking for whichever doctor or nurse has been attending him. He has a nasty graze on his cheek and his kneecaps resemble red apples. He's swaying left and right as if drunk, or woozy from painkillers. Heads turn in his direction but nobody seems concerned. The man slams his fist against a cupboard.

"Hey, you lot! I need a criminal doctor! I got kicked in the chest and I know who did it. I work in Italy. Came home two days ago and got beaten up. What do you think about that? I need a lawyer!"

An orderly offers a blanket. "Sir, put this on, you'll get cold."

"Back off, I don't need a fucking blanket!"

"Here, it'll keep you warm." The orderly drapes the blanket around the man's shoulders and it has a calming, almost magical effect until the orderly asks him to sit and wait. The man flings the blanket to the ground and struts about in his underwear.

"You lot! Yes, you lot, you doctors at the table! I want a criminal doctor to write this down. I got booted in the chest. I could hardly breathe. I know who did it. I want to press charges!"

"Sir, please sit down and wait."

"Fuck off! I've waited too long. Call this a hospital?"
"Sir–"
"Shut your fucking gob! You know what? Forget it. I beat myself up. Kicked myself in the chest. Yeah! I'm going home!"

He spins on his heel, heads for the door, and finds it eventually.

"Angela Nicoară?" A handsome young doctor approaches us, holding some documents, including a green form, possibly the one Angela filled in when we arrived. Perhaps he'll ask her what's wrong. On the other hand, he looks like he already knows.

"Well, madam, I'm happy to tell you, it's not appendicitis."

"They told me that at five-thirty. So, what is it?" asks Angela.

"We think it could be a little stone in your kidney, too small to see in the echo. So, we'll give you some pills. The urine test was just a summary; we recommend a second one after a few days, in case you have a urinary infection, but, actually, we don't think it's that. So, you can go home. Unless you have any questions?"

I resist the urge to ask if he can recommend a good nuthouse. Instead, we shake his hand, thank him very much, and walk along the grey corridor. Time to go home.

It's been a long day, but at least we know what the problem is and what it isn't. As for the medics, we can only be grateful, because they do their best against all the odds, are paid peanuts, and treated Angela free of charge. Besides, a friend of ours had to wait twelve hours for emergency care in super-duper Dublin, quite recently. Nor is Britain's health service so great these days, and we've lived in many countries where minor medical problems can spiral out of control in no time. Lost a few friends in those places, too, such as the dynamic American professor who complained of a sore back one Tuesday and was dead by the weekend. It happens to the best and brightest.

We plod downstairs, holding hands, and across the dark lobby. The friendly receptionist has closed her kiosk for the night. I hope she managed to sell all her nice blue bootees, even if nobody wore them.

Hrrrnnnh!

Don't take it personally, but this rumpled, middle-aged fellow shuffling along the dirt road will never speak to you. Greet him, and he'll respond with a rasping grunt at best. In time, after a few such encounters, he might offer a knobbly hand to crush yours, or curl his unshaven chops into a drooling smile to brighten your day. But, behind those deep-set, pale blue eyes, only he knows what's going on. You can ask, but he'll never tell. Inscrutable, that's the word. His wrinkled face resembles an ancient potato. His name is Gavril.

As a toddler, Gavril fell into a barrel of oil that scalded the hide off him and scared the wits out of him. He's never spoken about it, or about anything else, for the last sixty years. The tragic mishap rendered Gavril mute and somewhat retarded, if that's the word. Most of the time, he just wanders in a daze. As might we, if we were in his battered boots.

Not that Gavril is helpless; on the contrary, he's quite independent. Lives in a basement room, under the house occupied by his extended family, with his own front door, dusty windows, stove, sink, table, chair, bed, cupboards, wardrobe, and a bathroom out back. Compared to some other ageing and retarded mutes around the world, Gavril's lucky. Lucky he's not banged up in some godforsaken, state-run madhouse where the manager has a plasma TV in an office marked *Private.* Lucky to be alive, actually: what if Gavril had gone head first into the barrel?

Come wintertime, you'll encounter him plodding through the snow, huddled against a bitter wind and carrying a bundle of dead wood across his shoulders, arms outstretched, to secure it. *Christ, he looks like Jesus carrying the cross.* Gavril will grimace as you pass. *Was that a smile of recognition?* I'd like to think so.

Every spring, you'll find him lounging among the wildflowers and watching a small herd of munching sheep. If you sit nearby, he'll chuckle, as if to say, *What, you expect a conversation?*

For answers, you'd best chat with a member of his family, such as his sharp-tongued sister-in-law, Doamna Regina. She's one of the few people who can interpret Gavril's grunts.

Doamna Regina has more opinions than teeth, and will offer all sorts of advice anytime you don't need it. Like today.

She's standing in her favourite place, on the sloping path outside her house, hands behind her back, observing the not-very-much-goings-on. If our little village ever needed a community policewoman, she'd make a good one. Then again, our little village would first need to be a community. Alas, all too often, it's every Christian for themselves. Perhaps that's why Doamna Regina looks so dissatisfied, so often. Troubled, even. Like now.

She calls out to her brother-in-law. "What's up, Gavril?"

"Hrrrnnnh, hrrrnnnh!" He waves an arm and shuffles past her.

"Fine, as you wish," says Doamna Regina. Then she spots me, coming up the lane. "Wasting time again, Domnul Mike?"

"Hello, Doamna Regina, how do you mean?"

"Walking that fat dog of yours." Doamna Regina folds her arms, just above her distended belly. "Tie that dog up, I would. Dogs are tied up during the day and let loose at night."

"Not all dogs. You think Linda is fat?"

She gives me a look – *silly question, Domnul* – then frowns down the hill, at nothing in particular. "Chosen your *baba*, yet?"

"My what, Doamna Regina?"

"Your *baba*, it's already March, you must choose one."

"Right, during the first nine days or something?"

"Or *something?*"

"Angela did mention it, but I forgot."

"Well, I just reminded you. So, choose a *baba*."

"How about the seventh, is that ок?"

"As you wish, seventh of March." She lurches away. "Now I need to sit. Join me, if you're not too busy with that fat dog."

I should probably walk home, because it will be doggy dinnertime soon, and Linda knows it. But seeing as Doamna Regina knitted the brown woollen sweater I'm wearing today and the grey one I'll be wearing tomorrow, I feel obliged to accept her invitation. That's what friends are for, after all. So, I follow her up the path and I tie my dog to a tree. Linda whines but I raise my palm: *Hush now, sit.*

Doamna Regina settles on a rough wooden bench and pats the space alongside for me: *Sit*. I obey and ask her to clarify all this *baba* stuff.

"Stuff?" She makes a face and it's not very smiley.

"Sorry, Doamna Regina, all new to me."

"I can tell." She raises a finely-plucked eyebrow, and explains, as you might to a dim child, that the weather on your chosen *baba* day reflects your character and prospects. In other words, nice weather means you are decent and will enjoy a happy old age. Bad weather means you are somewhat crabby and surely doomed.

"So, which *baba* did you choose?" I ask.

"First of March, same every year."

"And was it a nice day?"

"Very sunny, Domnul Mike. Usually is."

"Must be true, then, Doamna Regina?"

She smirks, caressing her Brillo Pad hair, but won't be drawn, because one couldn't possibly comment on stuff like that.

Gavril ambles past us and waves at me. His ragged baseball cap has a frayed peak. He likes hats. That's why I remembered to buy him a smart tweed cap, two years ago, while I was visiting London. I remember coming here and giving it to Doamna Regina, nicely wrapped and tagged: *To Gavril, Happy Birthday!* What I don't remember is ever seeing that cap on Gavril's head. Instead, I saw some stranger wearing it – a friend of Regina's, as it turned out. Lesson learned. Next time I bring a gift for Gavril, I'll put it in his hand. Or on his head, where it belongs.

Gavril slumps onto a wooden bench and unties his left boot. He yanks it off to reveal a tatty brown sock. He looks a bit miffed, rubbing his foot. He removes his other boot, revealing a tatty green sock, and massages that foot.

"His feet are playing up," says Doamna Regina.

"What's the problem?" I ask.

"Toes, that's the problem. He hasn't got any. Not anymore."

"Because of the hot oil?"

"No, Domnul Mike, because of the frostbite."

"What happened?"

"His feet got cold."

"Well, yes, but how come? And when?"

Doamna Regina sighs. "Let's see, fifteen years ago? Midwinter, lots of snow. Gavril was home alone, the rest of us had gone shopping. Some village lads dropped by our house, with a bottle. They told Gavril about some girls at the shepherds' cabin in the mountains. Pretty girls who liked a drink and wanted boyfriends. It was all baloney, of course."

"I did wonder, that place closes every winter. And even in summer, no womenfolk are up there."

"Exactly, but Gavril never understands things like that. As far as he knew, pretty girls were visiting the shepherds. So, he says to himself: *I'm sort of a shepherd, I'm not getting any younger, I'd better get a move on.* Then, God help him, he sets off, all alone."

"Gavril walked to the shepherd's cabin in winter?"

Doamna Regina nods, wiping a tear. I turn away to gawp at mountains. Somewhere up there, in a wide valley, sits a big cabin of charred, waterproof logs. I've only been once, it's so far. Angela and I visited to buy cheese. The shepherds ferment it in hand-sewn tubes of pine bark. Wondrous place, the cabin. Reeks of woodsmoke, livestock, and stale milk. They keep dogs as big as the bears who come a-sniffing for free-range cows and pigs. For visitors like us, it's an eye-popping trip back to cowboy life, circa 1850. But what they don't have up there, is any women. Their wives and daughters stay home, down in the local villages, and as for pretty, local girls on the lash, no chance. As I recall, we walked six hours to get there, in July. *So, how long in winter?* It beggars belief. I can hardly believe my boots and they're good ones. Gavril's boots look like they were made from elephants' ears.

"So, that's how he got frostbite?" I ask.

Regina nods, blowing her red nose into a blue handkerchief.

"We came home from our shopping trip. *Where's Gavril?* We asked around but nobody knew. I stayed up all night, worried sick. Next morning, a cousin phones, a mountain ranger he was. By the grace of God, some of his colleagues had found Gavril curled under a tree, half-dead. They could tell from his tracks that he'd been walking around it, all night, probably to keep warm. But he'd given up. Look at him, see? Daft bugger knows I'm gossiping." Regina points a finger. "About you, yes."

I glance across the yard. Gavril is holding his boots. He looks happier now, grinning at us in the sunshine. *Who, me?*

A mangy moggy saunters between us and rubs itself against a tree trunk. It spots my Linda tied to the next one, and freezes.

"Our little skinny cat likes your fat dog," says Regina.

"Nine lives, just like your Gavril," I say, and we watch the pets' standoff. Linda is curious but wary. The cat plays hard to get.

"But, Doamna Regina, how did you find out about the village lads teasing Gavril with their baloney? Did he tell you that?"

"No, Domnul Mike, they told us after they heard Gavril was in hospital. Guilty consciences, I suppose. My brother Radu wanted to throttle them, but we were just glad to know the truth."

"So, the rangers took Gavril to hospital after they found him?"

"Yes, to Dumbrăvița. They told us he could easily die and they took him straight there. We drove down too, as fast as we could. The doctors told us Gavril might survive the hypothermia but they wanted our permission to amputate his feet: *Yes or no?* We didn't know what to say. Just imagine – Gavril without feet? Unable to walk or manage in his room, without our constant help? Gavril unable to tend our livestock, fetch wood, or even to pump water? Our life was hard enough already, so I told those doctors, *No, thanks, we'll take our chances.*"

"Chances of what?"

"Making Gavril better, of course."

"How did you intend to do that?"

Regina wobbles her head. "There are ways."

"To save frozen feet?"

She nods. "As soon as Gavril could sit up, we brought him home. I'd been looking in my grandma's remedy books, reading how to treat folks who get snowed up, about what would be good for feet – hawthorn, wormwood, aloe vera, and so on. I'd gathered my ingredients. I made my poultices and applied them day and night, week after week. Hard work, too."

"And?"

"Well, Gavril's toes dropped off but I saved his feet. Didn't I, you frisky bachelor boy?"

Doamna Regina wags a finger at Gavril. He sits rocking from side to side on the old bench, grinning and grunting. "Hrrrnnnh!"

Tyranny

The bell in the village church bongs a summons to the faithful and here they come, wearing their finest: kids, teenagers, middle-aged farmers with their wives, and three elderly women bent double because a long life becomes a heavy burden.

Angela and I stand back to allow the women to go first. Hunched over, clad in black, widows all, they plod up limestone steps worn smooth by generations of God-fearing folk. Reaching the top, they shuffle towards the little cemetery. We're here to honour a few of those already in it, and all of those who fell in some corner of a foreign field that will be forever Romania. It's Heroes' Day, same every year, on the fortieth day after Orthodox Easter. Neither public holiday nor religious feast, it feels like both. The kids get time off school to come and sing sad songs.

Two eager young boys in thimble-shaped straw hats try to jump the queue on the steps, but a stiff-backed, wrinkled fellow in a dark suit raises his shiny walking cane to block their progress. He doesn't speak, but his genial glare says it all: *Wait.*

The boys back down and scamper up a grassy slope instead, their baggy black pants and white cheesecloth shirts billowing in the breeze as they run. They find their friends and slap high fives. *Made it, just in time.* They stand and watch a group of teenage girls, pretty maids all in a row. The girls wear embroidered white blouses, black aprons, cute bonnets or ribbons, and a little make-up. Each of them clutches a posy of mixed wildflowers – buttercups, ragged robins, and margaritas – plucked from a meadow en route, no doubt. The boys inch closer to the girls, offering coy smiles and banter. It would make a nice photo. *Maybe later.*

First, we must pay our respects. Even the weather seems to be behaving itself, which makes a change. Let's hope the world is changing, too, and for the better. *Who needs war?* Time will tell.

We gather into a semi-circle before a monument of shiny brown marble about the size of a barn door. Etched with names and dates, it's a memorial to the fallen of two world wars. Some of them sided with tyranny but, in the end, most of them stood up to it, and that's why we're standing here today.

The priest recites long prayers, and chants mournful litanies to the dead. Birds contribute a chorus from silver birch trees. A grim-faced fellow in a woolly jumper swings a silver pot of incense and sweet-smelling smoke wafts over us like a magic spell.

The villagers make the sign of the cross – once, twice, three times. I bow my head and muse on the poor souls under our feet, who perished in conflict. I reflect on the good fortune of my own generation: how did we manage to slip through the cracks in history and avoid the countless bullets, bombs, and bayonets?

Staring at bright green grass between my feet, I think about my parents, as kids, living through the Nazi's blitz of Liverpool. How they would huddle overnight in dark, dank air-raid shelters, then, in the morning, hurry along shattered streets to find out which friends and neighbours had been blown to bits. *Imagine that.* I whisper to my wife, "What do we know about anything?"

Angela nods in silent accord and raises a finger to her lips.

The service ends and the gloomy atmosphere lifts. Little kids romp around the cemetery while their grandparents lay flowers at the memorial or kneel in private prayer at a sunken headstone. Angela drifts away to greet some neighbours, and I photograph chattering teenagers in traditional costumes as they clamber aboard a horse-drawn cart. Sounds like they're off to a party. Next, I snap the three elderly widows cloistered in chat, then spot the old gent with the walking cane. He's talking with a friend and both have military medals pinned to their jackets. When I ask the men if I may take their photo, they click heels and stand to attention – shoulders back and chins up. It's a nice touch. *Snap.*

The taller fellow with the cane asks me if I'm German. His voice is hoarse and barely audible. I tell him I'm English but with Irish ancestors and a Scandinavian surname. He seems unconvinced. "Pass for a German, you would."

His colleague nods. "True, and I should know. I served in Operation Barbarossa, 1941. Know what that was, young man?"

I notice a speck of blood on his shaven neck. He's lucky to have a neck, after Barbarossa. "Germany's assault on Russia?" I reply.

"Top marks, son. We were on the wrong side for a while."

I'm not quite sure what to say about that curious detail of history, and they probably know the feeling. The taller fellow narrows his eyes at me, rotating his cane between his fingertips.

"And how about you, sir?" I ask.

"Stalingrad." That one word will suffice, and he knows it.

"Wow."

"Indeed," he says, shifting his weight as he explains, in a rasping voice, how the Third and Fourth Romanian army helped the Hungarians to protect flanks of the German Sixth, but the Russians launched Operation Uranus. I'm all ears. He's a history lesson on legs.

"Nineteenth of November, 1942, that was. Russians sent their Fifth Tank Army, and more. Pincer, like a crab." He raises a wiry hand, gesturing with two fingers. *Crab*.

The numbers spin my head. I gaze at his three medals, their lustre long gone and ribbons faded. "How old were you, sir?"

"Twenty-one years of age when the Soviets captured me. Captured thousands of us, actually. Brutes, they were. Brutes."

I try sums in my head. *He must be, what, around ninety-five?* Looks in amazing shape, considering. Clear-eyed and sharp-witted. Perhaps that's why he survived, when more than three hundred and fifty thousand Romanians did not, once the Russians got hold of them. That much I do know, because of chats with Angela.

I nod towards her and say, "My wife's grandfather was a prisoner of war in Russia. He walked home to Romania. He was a shepherd."

The taller man seems intrigued. "But not around here, I think?"

"No, *Tataia* was from Brăila county. He died in 1997."

"At least he was able to get home. And so must I. Good day to you."

"Thanks for your time. Nice photo, see?" I show them the snap, we shake hands, and they totter down the smooth steps.

Driving home with Angela, I remember something else. "Didn't your grandad eat dead dogs on his long walk home from Russia?"

"And dead horses."

Our friend Doamna Dița drops by our house, bearing a two-litre bottle of creamy milk fresh from Contessa, her beautiful cow with the doleful eyes. Angela stashes the milk in our fridge, and I fill the kettle.

"Tea, Doamna Dița?"

She nods, glancing around our home, as usual, as if to make sure. Of what, I'm never quite certain. She asks what we've been up to. We tell her about Heroes' Day.

Dița looks puzzled. "When was all that?"

"Last week. It was nice. Quite moving, actually."

"Uh-huh." She seems unmoved. Perhaps she'll tell us she survived the Allied bombing of Romania's oilfields at faraway Ploiești. Then again, as far as I recall, she's lived in these hills all her life. Her weather-beaten face is criss-crossed with lines, but her ice-blue eyes sparkle. She's frail but formidable. Eighty-six years old and still picking wild mushrooms in the forest, despite bears and boars. Lives alone and likes a joke, usually at your expense.

I sit alongside her, thumbing my phone. "Got some snaps, Dița, if you want to see."

She leans closer. I can smell livestock and hay. She tilts her head, peering at my photos. "Sunny, was it? Oh, there's little Gheorghe in a hat. And that young Miruna looks more like her mum every day. This picture of Alex in the cart is blurred."

Dița seems to know all the kids in the photos, perhaps because it takes a village to raise a child, especially when so many local parents are picking sprouts in Italy or mixing cement in Germany.

She points at my photo of kids climbing into a wooden cart. "Look at their lovely shoes, good for them. When I was that age, my mum bought me shoes but warned me not to break them! I had to go barefoot, most of the time."

I look towards Angela, who says, "No shoes, for these rough roads?"

"In the hills and mountains?" I add.

Dița shakes her head. "Shoes were for special days. Church, mostly. Maybe for a party."

"What about in cold weather?" I ask.

"Not nice. When I was tending our cows, my feet would get so cold, I'd have to put them in fresh cow poo, or even under a pissing cow, just to keep warm. Hard times we had, in them days, not like kids now. I was a what-do-y'call-it, domestic help, for a rich lady. Domestic slave, more like! She'd feed me *mamaliga* and onions, that was it. I'd be starving, most days. I'd steal plums from an orchard on the way home. Got a beating, one time, from the fellow who owned it. Kids today don't know they're born. Have you seen their gadgets? Oh, well, good luck to 'em, I say. I hope they had a nice party after singing at the church. Nice day, by the look of these photos."

Dița grunts approval, until I show her my prize shot of the two elderly men. She tuts, jabbing a bony finger at the taller fellow. "Him and his medals." She sits back and folds her skinny arms.

The kettle boils and I move away to make tea. Angela brings cups, saucers, and offers cake. Our guest shakes her head.

"No cake for me. But I wouldn't mind one of your nice chocolate biscuits, like last time, if you have any."

We do, and she eats several. But there's no such thing as a free Hobnob, even if you did bring fresh milk, so, after a few sips of Darjeeling, I show her, once more, the photo of the veterans.

"Doamna Dița, what did you mean, *Him and his medals?*"

She munches a biscuit. "Never mind that bossy old git."

"He fought at Stalingrad, did you know?"

"He was a brute, Domnul Mike, did you know?"

"At Stalingrad?"

"Here, in the village school. My teacher, he was."

"Really?"

Dița chuckles, munching away. *What do you know?* Angela dips a biscuit into her tea. Our guest watches, raising an eyebrow.

"Are we supposed to dip them, Doamna Angela?"

"If you like, that's what people do in England."

"Wouldn't know, I've never been. Doesn't the chocolate melt?"

"Not if you're quick. Like this."

Dița purses her lips, watching closely. "Now I get it." She dips a biscuit into her tea, then quickly out again. "Like that?"

Angela nods. "But don't try it with a scone."

Dița pauses, mid-munch. "With a *what*?"

I gaze again at the photo, baffled. "This fellow was a brute?"

Dița sighs. "Proper bully, aye. Terrorised us. Beat us with a ruler. Liked to grind his big hairy knuckles in my shoulder, just here. And he'd pinch the skin under our chins. It hurt so much, one girl would pee herself, all down her leg. He called her *Pișăcioasa – Little Pisser*. He'd mock her, *Let's ask Little Pisser, shall we?* She would cry her eyes out, all the way home. We hated school. No wonder I'm so dim. He should have stayed in bloody Russia. What are these biscuits called?"

Keep the Home Fires Burning

Hard to believe how time flies and people change. I scarcely recognise this tall, broad-shouldered young man clambering down from the train. Lugging a heavy rucksack, he scans the platform for a familiar face until he spots Angela, his aunt.

She waves at him and slithers through knots of people, sidestepping their bags. "Daniel, welcome!"

Her nephew appears weary, probably still tired after the long trip. The logo on his T-shirt looks familiar but I'm not sure why. His long shorts – or short longs – are presumably the height of fashion back home in New York. He's good-looking, sort of a young Elvis, and his black hair is gelled into spikes.

Last time I met Daniel, he was a cute toddler, trouble on legs, and living with his doting grandparents in the Romanian countryside. His mum and dad had emigrated to the United States when he was nine months old; he would join them eventually, as a four-year-old, and grow up in Queens. Now he's back – the prodigal mudlark – on his first trip home to the old country.

Romania has changed in the meantime and so has Daniel. He's older, wiser, and certainly bigger. Six feet three, even six-four? It's probably all them hamburgers.

He ambles towards me, a slow-moving fellow, no rush, no fuss, quietly confident, something of the bear about him. Maybe that's what life in the Big Apple does to a rural rookie – it's so fast and noisy that you retreat, hibernate, and emerge in your own sweet time?

"Welcome to Transylvania, Daniel, long time no see."

We shake hands.

"Yeah, man. Nice to be here, dope."

Despite his tired smile, he's got a strong grip. His accent will surely impress the local ladies as much as it might vex their men. Sauntering across the car park towards our little jeep, he tells me *dope* means *good,* and I'm relieved to hear it.

The ride to our mountain fastness is a slow one, as so often in summertime, mainly due to tourists who overestimate their driving skills and underestimate the potholes on this narrow, winding, dirt road. They careen around the hairpin corners – *what fun* – but invariably come a cropper when another car appears ahead of them doing exactly the same.

"Imagine the traffic if this road were asphalt?" says Angela, pumping the brakes.

It's a good point. Little wonder so many locals oppose the idea. We sit watching two Range Rovers inch past each other with only centimetres to spare. Daniel gazes at the tree-lined hills and updates us on his life across the pond. Actually, it seems he's juggling two lives: business studies at college plus a part-time job selling electronic cigarettes. And, just for good measure, he's got a foot in the door at a Manhattan real estate agency.

"That's the job I want most, after college. Maybe I should just quit college and, like, jump into real estate?"

"Don't quit college," says Angela.

"I guess not. Hey, do you guys, like, vape?"

"Do we like vape?" Angela glances at me.

"What's vape?" I ask.

Daniel chuckles. "I mean, do you smoke e-cigarettes? Do you vape? I brought samples. If you want to try some, that is."

When we get home, Angela leads Daniel to our guest room, or rather, to my study with a sofa-bed, and he seems pleased enough. He casts a glance at my guitars, and I ask if he still plays.

"Not much," says Daniel. "I was in a band but we never performed. The other guys got too nervous."

"That's a pity. Playing live is when you really learn."

Daniel selects a guitar, shreds a blistering solo, and says, "Hey, can I, like, vape on your terrace?"

"Be our guest, vape away."

Out on the terrace, Daniel gazes left and right, taking in the view of rolling valleys, dense forests, and distant peaks.

"Wow, it's unreal, like some dream. Remember that movie, *Truman Show*, where everything is perfect but actually fake? That's how this looks. I mean, like, these mountains? All this could just be a painting on a screen. Or it's like some curtain I could pull back."

"Is it *dope?*" says Angela

Daniel flashes a grin. "Word."

"Word?"

"It means, *You said it, that's the right word.*"

Daniel reaches into his knapsack and takes out a little gadget. It resembles an oversize fountain pen with a central section of glass. He sucks at the narrow end. The gadget makes a gurgling sound, then Daniel exhales a plume of sweet-smelling smoke. Actually, it's vapour. Daniel is vaping. And we are watching. He offers us the gadget but we decline like two middle-aged bores.

Over a candlelit dinner, we talk old times, recounting episodes from Daniel's childhood in the sticks. Or rather, Angela and I talk, while Daniel listens. He seems increasingly bemused as the anecdotes bubble up from our memory pot.

He forks his pasta, and says, "No way. I did *what?*"

"Got mad when we cut your hair," says Angela.

"Me? How come?"

"You'd spend your days mucking around outdoors with your friends, but when your grandparents tried to wash you, or even trim your hair, you'd just shriek. Anyway, we visited one time and cleaned you up."

"And I got angry?"

"Screamed the house down. Didn't want pyjamas."

"Because you slept in your clothes, usually."

Daniel shoots me a glance. "No way."

"Yes way," says Angela.

Daniel groans. "This is too embarrassing."

"Don't worry," I say, "we were all kids, once. I was a chatterbox even before I could talk, apparently."

"And I used to sleepwalk," says Angela, "even down the street, sometimes."

Daniel shrugs. "My childhood here is a just blur."

"How does it feel to return to Romania, at twenty-one?"

Our guest sits back, his thumbs interlocked. "Well, I guess it was kinda strange in Bucharest last week because I don't know that place. But I made some new friends. Mom had phoned their parents from New York before I left, so that was good. Now, I feel at home. I'm connecting, I guess?"

Angela raises her glass. "To Romania, your home from home."

We toast the old country and Angela and Daniel chat in their mother tongue. He speaks Romanian well for someone who left as a toddler. Me, I'm soon stranded in No Man's Language, where stuff makes sense but not very much because it's family talk. Angela asks Daniel if he remembers picking grapes with Uncle Aurel. Daniel shakes his head, munching pasta. He tells her about his earliest memories, and she looks puzzled to hear them.

I swirl red wine around my glass, watching the colours in candlelight. *What's my earliest memory?* Ah yes, I'm sitting under an ironing board, playing with plastic soldiers. Mum is steaming the laundry. We're listening to the radio. I hear a tune that makes my hair stand on end. The singer sounds like he wants to kill someone, possibly me. I feel scared but excited by the irresistible call of a bigger world beyond our garden gate. Mum says the song is *Twist and Shout*, by The Beatles. She tells me that they're a new pop group, and one of them lives near my auntie. I feel older and wiser, somehow. *Connecting,* as Daniel might say. But by the end of the song I'm a nervous wreck, clutching my soldiers.

Daniel sleeps late next morning and enjoys a leisurely breakfast on our terrace, sipping coffee and puffing vapour that smells of chocolate and cherries.

Around noon, we set off for a long hike into green hills. Daniel enjoys the panoramic views at the top but seems to find the descent hard going. I suppose he's used to the concrete canyons of Manhattan, not these steep slopes of snatching grass and treacherous clefts.

Reaching a shady grove in a gentle valley, we stop for a picnic of crusty bread, cheese, tomatoes, and more.

I notice Daniel's T-shirt. It's a different colour but has the same logo as the one he wore yesterday. "Is that the clothing brand you launched in high school?" I ask.

Daniel reaches for an olive. "Sure is, we put out three lines of hoodies and four lines of T's. Sold every one. But that was then."

"How's the company doing now?"

"It ain't. Friends and business don't mix, right?"

"Right. We've been there, done that, didn't get the T-shirt."

"Is that, like, a joke?"

"Yes and no. We went into business with a friend. Big mistake."

Angela tugs at bread. "How were your friends in Bucharest?"

"OK," says Daniel, "they want me to stay in touch, anyways."

"Are they into business? That could be interesting."

"I doubt it. They just want a boyfriend, sort of."

"Even more interesting. Is the boyfriend anyone we know, sort of?"

"Me, I guess. But there's five of 'em, so it's kinda awkward. They're friendly girls and all, giving me

175

their email, phone numbers, Facebook, and stuff. I'm like: *Uh, ок.*" Daniel frowns into the tub of hummus. "Can I put tomato with this stuff, on bread?"

"If you like," says Angela. "So, you've got *five* girlfriends?"

"Sort of." Daniel spreads hummus.

"After two days in Bucharest?"

"Yup. Can you pass me a tomato, please?"

Angela obliges. "Which girl did you like most?"

Daniel slices the tomato. "Well, here's the thing. None of them is my type, but then again, I'm not sure what my type is. Not yet."

He props himself on an elbow, gazes at his sandwich and demolishes it in a few bites. *Ravenous.* He's a big lad and it was a long walk. We sit listening to the birds and the bees.

"Your type is out there somewhere, Daniel," says Angela.

"Heading your way like a ship in the night," I add.

Daniel wipes his mouth on a paper napkin then sits upright, patting his pockets.

"Forgot my vape."

We're exhausted when we get home and slump into whicker chairs on the terrace. The sun dips behind the mountains and we pull on warm tops. The sky darkens from ruby to purple and a crescent moon smiles down. Winking stars invite us to ponder universal mysteries, but it's getting cold, so maybe some other time. We retreat indoors and Daniel squats at our wood burner, hoodie up and arms folded.

"Can we, like, make a fire?"

"Dope idea, Domnul."

I reach for a box of matches, open the little glass door of the burner and strike a light. The tiny flame licks a scrap of paper and ignites a bunch of dry twigs under a stout log. The fire is roaring soon enough and we settle in armchairs, each with a purring cat in our lap.

There's something about fires – something reassuring, and yet not, because they warm and they warn: *Enjoy me while you can; time will pass, and what seems substantial will soon reduce to ash.* Such is life. We come and we go, like fire. Log in, log out.

Around 10 p.m., Angela glances up from her Kindle. "Bed, Mike?"

"Dope idea, Doamna." I close my paperback, stifling a yawn.

"Let's look in on Daniel first," says Angela, "he's been very quiet since dinner."

"Tired from our walk and the fire made him sleepy, I expect."

"Sure, but let's just see if he needs anything."

We walk across the room and into the hall. The door of my study is slightly ajar, casting a shard of bright light towards us. I reckon our guest is still reading. Or perhaps he's texting five lovestruck young ladies back in Bucharest.

Angela knocks gently. No reply. She pushes the door with her foot and we peep into the room. Daniel is stretched on the sofa bed, mouth agape and fast asleep. He's still wearing his baggy shorts, T-shirt, and Nike trainers.

"Some things never change," whispers Angela.

"Shall we cut his hair?" I whisper back.

"Don't be a dope, Mike."

"Word."

I reach through the gap, turn off the light, and we retreat as quietly as we can, just like old times.

Dog for a Dog

Doamna Irina looks sad. *Worried, even?* Something, anyway. Tired eyes gaze from her wrinkled face. She's standing in the vegetable patch outside her little wooden cottage, on the steep slope beside the dirt road, as we drive past. Her headscarf is tied tight and her faded pinafore flaps in the wind. She grips a walking stick to support her frail body. It can't be easy living in this remote spot, on a pittance, at her age. She waves at us, her palm horizontal, moving up and down, the Romanian sign language for *stop, please.* Perhaps she needs bread, some bananas, maybe a beer for her ailing husband, from the supermarket in town.

"Slow down," says Angela, from the passenger seat. I squeeze the brakes and lower my window, shielding my eyes from the sun.

Doamna Irina waddles down the slope and rests a brown hand on the grey fence.

"Domnul Mike, do you want a pup?"

"A pup?" I turn to Angela, and we shake our heads. *No way.*

"Sorry, Doamna Irina, but we have enough pets already."

"Oh, well, just thought I'd ask. My little Reta gave birth three weeks ago. I've been watching out for you ever since, Domnul Mike."

"Reta had pups? I didn't even know she was pregnant."

"Neither did I, but she was. Under that tatty coat of hers, eh? Needs a good trim. I've tried but she won't let me."

Angela leans across me and calls up the hill. "Doamna Irina, we can put some photos on Facebook, if you like?"

Doamna cups a knobbly hand to her ear. "Do what?"

I check my watch. We have time to spare. "Can we come up to your house for five minutes, Doamna Irina?"

She looks somewhat intrigued.

The pups are in Doamna's barn, around the back of the ramshackle house, just beyond her ramshackle ram. Two yipping balls of white fluff, they wobble across the grassy floor to gnaw at our fingers, *grrr*. Taking their photos proves difficult, however, because the pups won't sit still and their mother keeps pawing at our shins: *Me, me.*

Doamna grins down. "Reta thinks you've brought food."

I shake my head. "Not today, Reta, sorry."

"Used to bark at you, every day, this one, remember?"

"Drove our dogs crazy. That's why I started feeding her."

"First time I saw you throwing food to Reta, I thought, *What's that fellow up to?* But now look. She knows you. Both of you."

"Sweet girl, aren't you, Reta?" says Angela.

The tiny white dog wags her tail. Wags something, anyway. Reta would win no prizes for her looks. Sometimes you can't tell which end is which. You can't even see her face, for a start, because it's hidden under a web of long, mucky dreadlocks, just like the rest of her. They sprout and dangle from her ears, legs, belly, you name it. If you found Reta in a rubbish dump, you'd rescue the rubbish dump. She needs a trim, indeed. After a visit to the launderette. You could use the *Wool Wash* setting. Twice, probably. Doamna Irina beams with pride.

"Hungarian Terrier, or so my daughter told me."

"You have a daughter?" says Angela.

"In Bucharest, yes. Suzi's a lawyer, sort of. Reta is her dog."

"So, why does Reta live with you?" I ask.

Doamna Irina has no answer. *Asta e.* That's how it is.

I hold the pups steady. Angela takes a few snaps on her phone.

"That should do. We'll put your pups up for adoption, online."

"But how much will that cost, Doamna Angela?"

"It's free. Facebook. Question is, how much do you want?"

"Nothing, I just want them off my hands. I can't feed them."

"You should ask for money, Doamna Irina."

"Why, Domnul Mike? If they're free, people will want them."

"Yes, perhaps, but who and why?" says Angela. "We took some pups to Bran market last year. Couldn't give them away. So, we put them online, free. Got some strange calls. Best ask for decent money, that way decent people will want them. But it's up to you."

Doamna Irina pinches her lower lip between finger and thumb, making it pucker all pink. "Fifty lei each?"

"Let's say a hundred each. Hungarian Terriers, yes?"

"Yes. Do you want a dozen fresh eggs for your trouble?"

"No trouble," says Angela.

"But perhaps you should get Reta sterilised," I add.

Doamna Irina tugs again at her lip. "How much would that cost?"

"We'll ask and let you know. Lovely pups, by the way."

Doamna gives me a look as if to say, *So, why don't you take one?*

The moment we post photos of the two tiny Hungarian Terriers on Facebook, they attract attention. *Thumb, thumb. Like, like.* Fifty in fifteen minutes? Angela and I scroll through adoring comments, top to bottom. Several people want the pups but when we say *Come to Culmea,* they back off, one by one.

Culmea's too far.
Never Mind.
WTF?

We get lucky in the end, though. A young woman in Cluj offers to travel ten hours, by overnight train, to collect both pups.

One for me, and one for Dad as a surprise. It's his birthday soon. His terrier died.

Angela keys in our response. *Lidia, mulțumesc, but you'll have to wait another month, so these two can wean.*

Lidia agrees. It's a deal. It's also time to phone Doamna Irina with the good news.

Three days before Lidia is due to arrive, we drop in on Doamna Irina to finalise arrangements. She leads us to the musty barn. The pups are bigger but less goofy and scoot under a wheelbarrow, eyeing us from the gloom. Reta paws our shins: *Bring any grub?*

"We'll collect the pups on Saturday at noon," Angela tells Doamna Irina, "and drive them down to the train station. When Lidia arrives, on the one o'clock, we'll give her the pups, get the two hundred lei and bring it to you. How does that sound?"

Doamna Irina doesn't answer. She looks a bit worried, or a bit sad, as so often. Her tanned face is all ridges and wadis like an Arabian desert in miniature. She gazes down at the cowering pups. One of them whines. *What?* Perhaps it senses change in the air.

I couch beside the wheelbarrow and reach under it, to caress their fluffy paws. "Don't worry, Doamna Irina, these pups will be OK. I'll bring strong cardboard boxes with holes for ventilation."

"And Lidia seems very nice," adds Angela, "so, we're sure her father is decent, too. These little ones are going to good homes."

The pups emerge from their hiding place, all ears.

Doamna Irina sighs. "My daughter says it's not enough."

"Not enough what?"

Doamna Irina breaks her studied silence. "Not enough money, Doamna Angela. Suzi phoned last night. She wants five hundred lei each, because they're

Hungarian Terriers, after all. Suzi said they belong to her. Reta is her dog. I'm just minding it, Suzi said."

Angela and I look at each other, then at the pups. They're at our feet, belly up, grinning with tiny teeth. *We're Hungarian Terriers, after all.*

Angela shakes her head. "Doamna Irina, we agreed *one hundred* each. We told Lidia a month ago. That was the deal. You can't change the price at the last minute, that's not fair."

"Suzi says it's not enough. These pups belong to her, after all."

"So why didn't Suzi handle the adoptions?" I ask.

"She was too busy. That's why I asked you. You like dogs."

"But we don't like being messed around, Doamna Irina."

"Neither will Lidia," says Angela.

"So what do I do?" Doamna Irina slumps onto a bench and looks at the rafters. But there are no answers up there, only cobwebs.

Angela sits beside her. "Phone your daughter, today, and tell her, *one hundred each*. Or we're out. And we'll tell Lidia why."

Doamna Irina gazes down at her battered boots. "Very well, but my phone has no credit." She pulls an old Nokia from her dusty pinafore and wipes the dusty screen, as if this might help.

"Use mine," says Angela, "what's your daughter's number?"

Doamna Irina is soon chatting away. *Bună, Suzi, ce faci?*

Saturday comes and we drive across the village with two empty cardboard boxes on the back seat of our car.

They're nicely ventilated and lined with sweet-smelling, dry grass, because a deal is a deal and this one is still on. Until we get to Doamna Irina's. She emerges from the barn, carrying a fat white pup.

"And the other one?" I ask, rolling down the window.

"It's not here. My daughter drove up late last night from Bucharest. She left this morning. She took the other pup."

"She did what?"

"Asta e."

Angela slides from the car. "Doamna Irina, Lidia's on the overnight train from Cluj. Do you know how far that is?"

"Far."

"Three hundred kilometres. For two pups. Did you tell your daughter?"

"Yes, of course, but Suzi said, *Reta is my dog and this is my pup.* I wanted to phone you, Doamna Angela, but… no credit."

"You couldn't borrow Suzi's phone?" I ask.

Doamna Irina shakes her head. "Suzi was in such a bad mood, I didn't even dare to ask. Anyway, here's a pup for your friend."

Lidia from Cluj is petite, well-dressed, and good-looking, with dark eyes and olive skin. Dazzling smile, too, despite her night on a train. She steps onto the platform, *Hello, there!* We open the cardboard box and she lifts out the fluffy pup.

"My goodness, what a beautiful little doggy you are!"

"Smells of sheep, sorry, Lidia," says Angela.

"Oh, a nice warm bath will soon fix that. And the other pup?"

We tell Lidia that it's in Bucharest, and then we explain why. Her happy smile fades. She gawps at us, fit to weep. *Bucharest?*

"Sorry," I say.

"We tried our best," says Angela, "truly we did."

Lidia stands quietly for a few moments, shaking her head. There's little else we can add. She shrugs, tight-lipped.

"Not your fault, folks. That's how some people are. Never mind. I'll give this pup to my dad and find one for me another time, perhaps."

She looks down the track. It will be a long ride home.

Doamna Irina phones us a week later because she has credit. Angela puts the call on speaker and we listen, somewhat warily.

"Is everything OK, Doamna Irina?"

"Suzi says no more pups. They're a bit of a nuisance."

"Quite right," says Angela, with a wry smile for me.

"So, can you fix her?"

"Fix who?" I ask.

"Fix Reta. I can use the money you gave me, Suzi said."

I lean towards the phone. "Wouldn't she prefer to handle this herself, seeing as Reta is her dog, after all? Perhaps the next time Suzi visits from Bucharest, she could take Reta to our local vet?"

"Too busy. She's a lawyer, sort of. Spends a lot of time in court."

"I can imagine."

I drive down the winding forest road to our favourite vet in Dumbrăvița and plop raggedy-arsed Reta on his stainless steel table. Cosmin stares at her, then at me.

"This is a dog?"

"Hungarian Terrier, apparently."

"Crossed with what, a fucking octopus? Just my luck. What a mess. Name?"

"Reta."

Cosmin rubs the dog's head. "Reta, you're a disgrace."

Reta wags her dreadlocks. *Tell me about it.*

When she returns from the Land of Nod to the little wooden cottage on the hill, Reta looks like a different dog. Transformed from unspeakable wretch to sleek terrier. *West Highland meets shorn Transylvanian lamb?* She totters around, groggy from the anaesthetic. Her eyes are glassy but at least you can see them now, all black and shiny like rare gems. Reta is almost cute.

"Snipped and trimmed," says Angela.

Doamna Irina clasps hands in joy. "Oh, so different!"

I show Doamna a photo on my phone. "And take a peep at this, from Lidia. Her dad loves his new pup. Named it Bobby. Doing well, see?"

The photo shows a spotless white Bobby sprawled on a red shag-pile rug and chewing an old tartan slipper.

Doamna Irina looks closer. "Nice chairs."

Next time I see Reta, she's trotting alongside our car and barking blue murder as we drive past. Talk about gratitude. But she does look lovely in the spring sunshine, and that's the main thing. No dreadlocks. No more unwanted pups. Reta is a new dog. Even Suzi might want her, one day.

Summer arrives, and with it, a steady stream of tourists in shiny cars, mostly at weekends, from all over Romania and beyond. Sometimes, we spot registration plates from Latvia, Poland, France, the works. Our little village is on the map, big time.

Doamna Irina is in her vegetable patch, wearing baggy pants with muddy knees. She waves down at us and looks worried.

"Let's stop and see what she wants," says Angela.

I squeeze the brakes and we stop. I lower my window, shielding my eyes from the sun. Doamna Irina waddles down the slope and rests a brown hand on the grey fence.

"Domnul Mike, Doamna Angela, have you seen my Reta?"

"No, why?"

"She's missing. More than two weeks, now."

Angela leans across me from the passenger side. "Oh dear, sorry to hear it, Doamna Irina. Where did you last see her?"

Doamna points her rusty trowel. "There, at the bend. A car stopped. They opened the door."

"They who?"

"Tourists, I think." She wipes her eye – grit or grief, it's hard to tell. "Nice car they had, anyway. They were feeding her. Reta had learned to beg, like this." Doamna raises her forearms, pawing the air. *Gimme gimme.* I try not to laugh. Her dog is missing, after all.

"And they took Reta?"

Doamna shrugs. "I think so, Domnul Mike. Perhaps they thought she was a stray."

It seems unlikely. A stray dog does not have a neatly-clipped coat with a cute bob at the end of her tail. More likely, Reta has been kidnapped. Stolen. *Dog-napped*. Not that we'll say so.

"Have you told your daughter?" I ask.

Doamna winces. "I don't dare. Anyway, I have no credit."

Angela pulls out her phone. Doamna Irina looks scared witless.

"No, Doamna Angela, I can't call Suzi! What would I tell her?"

"Just the truth, and it's not your fault."

"Suzi won't believe me. No, I'd prefer to wait. Dogs often disappear then come back a few days later. Weeks, even. Oh, well, just thought I'd ask. How are you for eggs?"

"Fine, thanks," says Angela.

"Pity about the dog," I add, "but we'll keep an eye out."

There's not much more we can do, so we drive on, around the bend in the dusty lane where Reta was last seen. Now she's gone.

"I hope she's not stuck in some tiny flat," says Angela.

"Me too, Reta belongs here, out and about on the hills."

"Who would steal her? Such a heartless thing to do."

Our thoughtful silence lasts only a few moments.

"I feel sorry for Doamna Irina. Suzi will give her hell, I bet."

"Probably, Mike, but what goes around, comes around."

"Meaning?"

"Meaning if someone took Reta, it was because they liked her. That's why they were feeding her, don't you see? Suzi didn't want her dog, not really. She didn't even want a pup, until–"

"Oh, no, Angela, I just realised."

"What?"

"This is my fault."

"Why is it your fault?"

"Because Reta was aggressive towards us."

"What?"

"I mean she was aggressive until I started feeding her. And then she was nice with us, always. Don't you see? That's it. I taught her that strangers can be a source of food. Now this. It's my fault."

"Mike, you were hardly a stranger. You became her friend."

"Some friend."

I drive slowly up the long hill, under a dappling canopy of dense green foliage. Shafts of sunlight stab my eyes and this damn road is bumpy all the way. Once upon a war, a thousand soldiers probably marched up here, sabres rattling. Now it's just us, and locals, and cars of bug-eyed tourists. Like the ones who nabbed a cute white terrier with a waggy tail?

"Perhaps they were Hungarians taking back what's theirs."

"Perhaps they were, Mike, but let's not get into all that."

We Are Not Alone

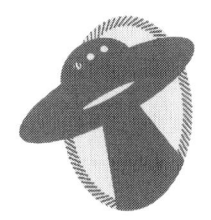

My wife spots it first. She pauses on our walk and points into the darkening sky. "What is *that*?"

I look up. A yellowish light flickers and flares as it passes over the village. Circular in shape, it moves at a steady speed – not too fast, not too slow.

"No idea. Bit weird, though. How high, do you think?"

"Could be a hundred metres, could be a thousand."

"Looks like it's ready to explode. Is it on fire, Angela?"

"Hope not. I'll take a photo."

She whips out her phone and points it at the sky. *Click.*

"Hear that noise, Angela?"

"It was my camera, Mike."

"Not that. It sounds like gas burning. Or a sparkler. Don't you hear it?"

"No, but this breeze is picking up. Maybe it was the leaves?"

"It's coming from that thing." I point at the glowing light.

"Whatever, let's get home before we break our necks on this road. Pitch black, soon."

We walk down the rocky lane, grasping the dogs' leashes, but they're not dragging us tonight; they're pacing slowly alongside, as if sensing our unease. I glance up.

"Still there, Angela."

The light is a faint speck soaring across the valley, towards the mountains. Then it's gone.

"You know what that was, don't you, Angela?"

"In Romanian, we say OZN. *Obiect zburător neidentificat.*"

"Exactly, we just saw a UFO."

According to the dictionary in my laptop, a UFO is *a mysterious object seen in the sky for which it is claimed no orthodox scientific explanation can be found, often supposed to be a vehicle carrying extraterrestrials.*

"Certainly mysterious," Angela says, at my shoulder.

"Noise was weird, too."

"I didn't hear it."

"Ever been in a hot air balloon?"

"No, Mike."

"Maybe it was a hot air balloon. That's how they sound. When you lose height, you turn a handle to release helium or something. A big flame shoots up, *whoosh.* Hot air fills the balloon."

"Nobody flies a balloon at night."

"Maybe it was one of those paraglider things on wheels. But, yeah, who would fly one at night? That can't be legal. Then again, this is Romania."

"Exactly. You forgot the local angle."

"The local angle?"

"Never mind definitions, search for locations. Use Google. Here, let me try."

I move aside and Angela types at the keys: *mysterious lights, Culmea, Brașov,* OZN, UFO. The screen fills with Romanian text.

"We're not alone, Mike. Someone else saw strange lights."

"Tonight?"

"Two months ago. Look, she posted photos like ours."

"Spooky or what. Write to her. Send the one you took."

Our neighbours differ in their reactions when we tell them we saw a light in the sky. Some offer tight smiles: *Yes, of course, you did.* Others listen and nod: *Yup, me too. Years ago, over there.*

The wrinkly-faced shepherd walking his flock up the lane reveals that he often hears the fairies – *iele-iele* – carousing on midsummer nights. They visit his fields. Mischief glitters in Domnul Octavian's tired eyes. He leans on his long stick and taps a fingertip at his long nose. "I can always tell!"

"How do you mean?" I ask.

"Because my grass is flat, Domnul Mike."

"Flat?" says Angela.

"From where the *iele-iele* dance with their little feet."

"Have you ever seen a strange light, like in this photo?"

Octavian cups a wrinkled hand over Angela's phone. "No, Doamna, but I know who has. Name's Dan. Lives way over there." Octavian points at distant hills.

"Do you have Dan's phone number?" I ask.

"I don't have a phone. If I want to talk to my sheep, they're right here."

We look at his sheep and they look at us. *Next question?*

"So, how do we find this Dan fellow?" says Angela.

"Walk to Dâmbu Vechi, turn left onto the goat track after the village, and go up the long hill. Dan lives on the top. In a strange house."

"Can we drive?"

"If you have a car. Yours is a nice one, I think?" Octavian grins, all gums.

Walking away, I remember that as a kid, if I lost a tooth, I'd put it carefully under my pillow and, next morning, find a shiny sixpence from the fairies. Given his connections with the *iele-iele*, I reckon our elderly shepherd must be minted by now.

The goat track is a bumpy, winding road. With no goats. They probably use an easier route. We drive forty minutes, reach the top, and spy a solitary house with a spectacular view of the surrounding mountains. We thought our home was in a nice spot, but this? *Holy moly.* Domnul Dan lives a stepladder from heaven. St Peter drops in to borrow sugar, probably.

The house is indeed strange. Long and wide, with a green, domed roof of rugged PVC, it seems to have grown organically from the earth, and looks like something a wealthy Hobbit might inhabit. Huge windows sparkle in the sun and the car park is snow-white gravel. *Classy.* We count six empty cars; some have Bucharest registration plates, some have Tulcea plates. *Visitors, in two groups?* We knock at the house. No reply. Not a dicky bird.

A tall, spindly sculpture stands nearby. The white column measures about five metres high and one metre in circumference. Solid white discs as big as car tyres are arranged vertically on the column and knobbly white spokes extend, like arms, from each disc. The sculpture resembles a totem pole festooned with giant snowflakes. Bonkers, frankly. We've come to the right place.

"What's this thing, Angela?"

"No idea. We'll ask Domnul Dan when we find him."

"*If* we find him. Looks like everyone's been abducted by aliens."

"There are people on the next hill, sitting in a big circle, see? Maybe he's up there with them, come on." Angela strides away.

"Slow down. What if it's some weird cult?"

"We don't join."

"Good luck with that."

We hike two hundred yards down a dip, up the next hill, and find the elusive Domnul Dan lounging at the top. He's barefoot on the grass, chatting to a dozen people who sit around him, at a respectful distance, listening closely. *The tourists, I reckon.* Certainly not local, judging by their cameras, bush hats, bandanas, and multi-functional cargo pants with tactical Velcro.

Dan is about sixty-five, with a tousled mop of silver hair. He's tanned and skinny, dressed in faded blue jeans and a white T-shirt. He looks like a retired rock star. He chews a grass stalk and has a quiet voice. Certainly charismatic. We've stumbled on an informal lecture, by the sound of it, about the importance of a healthy diet. We sit cross-legged to listen. Dan says he lives mostly on birch sap, whatever that is.

Noting our arrival, he pauses briefly to gesture with two fingers – *Peace* – then resumes his lecture, enthusing about goat cheese, clean living, and *being at one*. I can't hear him too well, given the blustery wind and his low-key delivery, but so far, so good. He takes questions. A woman wearing lots of beads asks to try birch sap. Dan points down to the house. *Sure, try before you buy.* I ask him about his totem pole.

"Actually, it's a message," says Dan.

"To whom?"

"To the lights in the sky."

"So, it's true, you've seen lights?" says Angela.

"Of course, Doamna, several times. Above our pyramid."

"Your pyramid?" I ask.

"Well, it's not like in Egypt. Ours is up there, see?" Dan points.

We crane our necks. Sure enough, high in the mountains, a huge pyramid of grey rock juts from a grass-lined gully. Well, sort of.

"Never noticed that before," says Angela, "it looks different from where we live. In Culmea, I mean. We saw a light, by the way."

Dan removes the grass stalk from his mouth. "You did?"

"In the sky over Culmea. A strange light. About a week ago."

"It's a message, I think." Dan flashes a Hollywood smile.

"What does your message on the totem pole say?" I ask.

"On my sculpture, you mean. Well, I hope it says, *I see you.* I designed it to replicate the lights in the sky. That's how they look. Round with spiky bits."

"Have the lights responded?"

"I believe so. I see them often. I consider that a response. There's energy around the pyramid. Some say it's just the weather—"

"The *weather?* Hah!" A pale-faced fellow in a threadbare black suit clambers to his feet, dusting dry grass from his pants. He walks about, wagging a finger. "Domnul Dan, these mountains were made by beings from ancient civilisations. I can prove it."

Heads turn. Eyebrows kink. Perhaps he's a guest lecturer.

"What sort of *beings?*" says a large man in khaki.

"Giants. You should visit my website."

The large man stares. *You should visit the nuthouse.*

Domnul Dan chuckles quietly to himself. I get the impression he's heard this lecture before. He shifts position and brushes the ground with his hand. He selects another grass stalk and inserts it into the corner of his mouth. Then he looks towards the pyramid.

Birch sap tastes like onion juice that has been poured through a giant's sweaty sock.

"Like it, Mike?" says our beaming host.

"Certainly refreshing, Domnul Dan."

"Fermented for seven years, hence the slightly bitter flavour. When you drink fresh birch sap, it tastes different to this, rather sweet in fact, like sugared water. I prefer my version. Either way, it's full of goodness and contains xylitol, amino acids, enzymes, proteins, all sorts. Birch trees have incredible healing properties. Peasants all over Europe have been drinking this for centuries. Cleanses the body. Natural detox for the kidneys, liver, and so on."

"Does aspirin come from birch trees?"

"No, willow trees. Oh, then there's Chaga mushrooms, of course. They grow on birch and are used in traditional remedies for cancer and other illnesses. We're surrounded by goodness."

I sip my bitter drink and smile sweetly. "You a doctor, Dan?"

"Just a chemist, retired. Now, drink up and follow me."

I drain my glass and wince at Angela. Hers is empty.

Dan leads us through a narrow, arched doorway and down rough steps into a large, circular cavern. *Either he's planning to induct us or abduct us.* The lime-washed walls are lined with shelves bearing huge demijohns of pale, cloudy liquid. *Birch sap, probably.*

Angela looks at a jar of white cubes. "Goat cheese?"

Dan nods, and offers us a sample. It tastes creamy, salty, and quite delicious. Bugger birch sap. We should buy this instead.

"How many goats do you have?" I ask

"Eighty. And their cheese is better for you than cow's cheese. Less lactose, you see, and richer in vitamins A and B. Full of calcium, phosphorus, iron, magnesium, potassium, and… oh, I forget."

"Isn't goat cheese high in fat?"

"The fat globules are smaller and easier to digest."

"Interesting."

"Riboflavin, that's the other thing. Now, let's go back upstairs and you can see my guest house."

We follow. I'm curious to have a look at Hotel Danifornia.

You can check in any time, but you can never leave without trying the birch sap.

Back upstairs, Angela buys a jar of goat cheese from Dan's little café, and he leads us outside. At the door,

I spy a line of seven beautiful grey furs hanging from hooks. Foxes, once upon a hill.

Dan leads us across his fruit and veg patch, offering tasty titbits en route: blades of peppery rocket, a handful of delicious strawberries, and a herb that I've never tried before. It's bittersweet, like sugar mixed with salt and a hint of lemon juice.

"Wow, what's this, Dan?"

"We call it *măcriș,* but in English, you call it sorrel."

Our host skips barefoot across the rough earth, happy as a kid. He moves with an easy grace, like a yoga guru. Talk about healthy.

The guest house is smaller than the main residence, but with similar decor – modern meets medieval – presumably by J.R.R. Tolkien. In fact, this whole place would make a perfect location for a *Ring* movie, if you like that sort of stuff. Dan is in his element. Me, I'm drifting back in time to a balmy evening in Singapore, many years ago, when a Frodo-loving American colleague dragged me to the première of the first film. He loved it. I walked out after ten minutes and broke the spell of our friendship. From then on, he referred to me as *Orcs*by.

"Is the guest house open for business?" Angela says.

"Soon, yes." Dan glances around at bumpy walls rag-washed bright pink. I just hope he can sort out that bumpy road. Talking of which, it will soon be time for us to wobble back down it.

We stand in his gravel car park, admiring the views.

"So, how much of this land do you own?" says Angela.

Dan shrugs. "Pretty much everything you can see."

Given that we can almost see New Zealand from up here, I'm increasingly curious about how *just a chemist* got so wealthy, but it would be rude to ask. Perhaps Dan saw a chance when land was cheap. Maybe he's the head of a pyramid scheme, funded by angel investors. Whatever. Perhaps I should start living on goat cheese marinated in birch sap.

Finally, lest we forget, Angela shows Dan her photo of the mysterious light. He strokes two fingers across the screen of her phone to expand the image, and looks closer. "Yes, the same."

"Same what?" says Angela.

"Spikes. The lights I see above the pyramid are round, with spikes, like these in your photo. I told you, I designed my sculpture to replicate them." Dan turns, pointing. "See?"

We nod. Now we get it. And he gets messages back.

"Actually…" Dan pulls a phone from his pocket and flicks through a gallery of shots: goats in pens, happy clients in his juice cavern, and po-faced people gathering pebbles into deep and meaningless mounds up the hill. Eventually, he finds the photo he wants.

"Look, this one."

We lean in. The photo shows a bright disc of jagged light slicing the gloom above a rocky peak. It glimmers and shimmers – purple, red, and yellow – like lasers at a pop festival. But there are no festivals in these remote mountains. Dan shows us more photos of the same light from different angles: a cosmic circular saw.

Angela tells him about the woman online. "She's got photos like yours. I sent her mine. I was hoping she'd reply, but…"

"Oh, well, please let me know if she ever does," says Dan.

"Got any photos of giants?" I ask.

"No luck so far," he says, with a grin.

"So, you really think the lights are sending a message?"

"You tell me." Dan offers us a gentle smile and a firm handshake. *Bye, neighbours.* We swap cards and take our leave.

Driving down the goat track, Angela and I don't say much. Because it makes you think.

Watching stars in a black sky and nibbling tasty goat cheese on our terrace, we agree on three things: Dan's birch sap tasted sour, birch sap is probably very good for you, and if the strange light was a message from extra-terrestrials, it's a nice one.

"Should we make a totem pole, and reply, Angela?"

"No, Mike, but open a bottle of wine, in case they drop in."

Finding Solomon

The first time I see Solomon, his name is not Solomon. He's just a dog – a big, mangy, fluffy white dog wobbling around the forest road. I'm driving to the railway station but that poor mutt is going nowhere. His stump of ear suggests that he's a working sheepdog, or was, once upon a pasture, where some shepherd cut off the rest. Now he's just a mess, falling apart. He's come for water from the gushing spring.

The three hikers filling their bright metallic bottles hardly give him a second glance. Perhaps they think he's got a disease, and who could blame them? That dog looks like he's got everything and nothing. I stop the car and roll down my window. Curiosity won't kill me and neither will he because I'm not a cat. I'm just interested.

First, I notice a bloody hole the size of a golf ball in his back leg. Next, the wound in his front paw, the gash in his head, and the muddy dreadlocks dangling from his back end. He's reed thin, ready for the knacker's yard, dead dog limping. But what I notice most is the look in his intelligent eyes: *Won't somebody help?*

I have no answer, just places to go and my wife to meet. I drive on with a heavy heart and a guilty glance in my mirror. The hikers amble into the forest and the dog stares at an uncertain future. He looks like a polar bear who had a fight. And lost.

"Need to collect my reading glasses," Angela says.

I park near the optician's and she hops out. I turn up the CD – *Best of Jazz*. It's Glenn Miller and he's *In The Mood*. But I'm not, so Glenn Miller can get lost; then again, he already did.

Angela returns and says, "I have to come back in half an hour. Fancy a coffee up the road?"

"Not really."

"Why the long face, something I said?"

"No, something I saw." I tell her about the big dog all bashed to bits. "He'll die, I bet. This winter. Slowly and painfully."

"Mike, we don't need another dog, I'm sorry, but–"

"We could at least take him to the vet."

"But then what?"

"Then I'll put him back where I found him."

"Fine, let's help the dog, then you put it back."

The dog is standing in the exact same spot when we pull up. His tail twitches as I approach with half a sandwich, donated by Angela. I break off a chunk, drop it on the ground, and the dog gobbles it up. Next, I offer a clenched fist. *Never fingers.* The dog sniffs my hand. So far, so good. Big brown eyes blink at me through a thatch of tangled white fur. *Got any more, Mister?*

I show him the rest of the sandwich. He wags his tail and licks his shiny black lips. I walk to the car, open the rear hatch, place the sandwich inside, and beckon him.

"Come on, Fleabag, hop in."

He stays put. *Hop? I can hardly walk.*

I walk back and caress his stumpy ear. "What if I lift you, big boy?"

Angela leans from the car. "What if he bites?"

"He won't because he knows I'm helping. I hope."

The dog is tall – just under a metre high at the head – but remains docile as I cup my forearms under his torso. Luckily for skinny boy me, he's badly underweight due to malnutrition, so I scoop him easily into the back of the car, where he wolfs the rest of the sandwich. Gone.

Driving back to town, I remember something important.

"Angela, could you call Cosmin and tell him we're coming?"

Our handsome, ever-helpful young vet rises from his chair. Cosmin is wearing a green smock, smart jeans, and red and yellow New Balance trainers. He gawps at my furry new friend.

"Angela said *a dog*. What the fuck is that?"

"It's a dog."

"Where did you find it, in a bin?"

"By the spring near the gorge. Can you help?"

"What am I now, a magician?"

"You're the best vet around."

"True." Cosmin circles the dog, shaking his head and whistling in despair as he inspects festering wounds and nasty lacerations. "Bitten to bits. Been in a fight. What a wreck."

Despite his reservations, Cosmin loves a challenge and knows we know it. His grimace mutates to a grin.

"Let's get to work!"

He administers a sedative and the dog slumps to the floor in a ragged, stinking heap. He looks like something the cat would not drag in. We raise him onto the stainless steel table where Cosmin injects a general anaesthetic and the doggy's tongue slithers out like a slice of ham.

"Now I'll shave him, just a bit." Cosmin uses his buzzing Remington Mutt Razor to shear off muddy dreadlocks, which I tip into a plastic bag. By the time we're done, the dog is as clean as a rusty whistle and the plastic bag weighs two kilos, easy.

"So, Mike, what's your dog's name?"

"Fleabag, but he's not my dog."

"Actually, he has no fleas, just wounds, some with worms, see?" Rubber gloved, Cosmin fingers the mushy hole in the back leg and extracts wriggling maggots. "Look, disgusting or what?"

I peruse maggots. "Hmm. Have you seen *Gladiator*?"

"Yes, why?"

"The worms in Russell Crowe's wound cleaned it up."

"That was then. Now we do this, watch." Cosmin sprays the dog's injuries with turquoise stuff from an aerosol can and soon our fluffy Fleabag resembles a priceless Picasso.

"Is that stuff antibiotic, Cosmin?"

"Clever boy, you should be a vet."

"I always wanted to, as a kid, until I found out you need good grades in science. I couldn't get them."

"Well, today you can be my assistant. Hold this leg."

I hold this leg while Cosmin threads transparent twine into a circular needle and sews up a gooey purple wound, good and tight. He's quite an artist.

"You're an artist, Cosmin, just like Picasso."

"Next, I'll do this hole under his jaw. That's a nasty bite. I reckon your dog was attacked by several others, all over."

"He's not my dog. But what about this long gash on his head? That's not a bite. Someone whacked him on the head."

"Maybe a shepherd got angry with him."

"Half an ear, did you notice?"

"Of course, they did that when he was a pup. Most of those shepherds have half a brain. Sadistic idiots. Seen the tail, Mike? The end is almost bitten off. I'd better sew that, too. Poor Fleabag."

Cosmin works for an hour, inserts twenty-five sutures but declines our offer of payment.

"Because it's not your dog, Mike."

"It's not yours either," says Angela, and we haggle for a bit.

Cosmin agrees to let us cover costs. "But my labour is free."

What a gentleman. Cosmin removes his rubber gloves and we his shake hand.

"Mulțumim."

"Cu plăcere," says Cosmin, "Fleabag will survive."

"I'll have to feed him up, he's way too skinny."

"Sounds like he's your dog, after all, Mike?" Cosmin shoots me a knowing look. I glance at my wife, hoping against hope.

Angela raises an eyebrow and says, "He's manky but cute, I suppose."

"You mean the dog?" says Cosmin.

Driving home, Angela and I agree that we can't possibly put Fleabag back where I found him because he's still unconscious, wheezing in his sleep in the back of the car. And we can't keep him because we have two dogs already – Linda the Rottweiler cross-breed and Sam the wannabe Husky. Not to mention our five cats and what if he attacks them, *etcetera.*

"So, what will we do?" says Angela.

"We'll keep him for a bit. Just until he's fit and well."

"Then what?"

I shrug as if I don't know. But I do know and Angela knows I know. I think the only person who doesn't know is Guess Who, but he'll find out when he wakes up.

My wife sighs, gazing out at the mountains. "You always wanted a big sheepdog, Mike."

"Did I, Angela? Oh, well, perhaps it's destiny. How are your new glasses, by the way?"

"Fine, I can see things very clearly now."

Someone Else

Decent watering hole, this. The young barmen are quick, polite, and know their football. Sharp-witted, too, and with good English. We trade banter and hope to see goals on the television. It's a long drive down from our mountains but I quite like being in Brașov, and this is a good place to stop off and catch a game on my way home. Well, until the bearded, beer-bellied Brit turns up.

Let me tell you about Andy, briefly. Before Andy tells me about Andy, at great length. He's a construction consultant in his late fifties, who arrived in Transylvania a few months ago. He can't decide whether to stay or go, and he loves to tell me why. Spins me the same saga every time we meet, while sipping his favourite bourbon or draught beer. I'm his new best mate, occasionally, whose name he can never remember.

"Mick," says Andy, settling in beside me, "I'll tell you what, there's so much potential in this country, but I'm fed up with being ripped off. Should I set up a business or leave? I can't decide."

Andy orders a double Jack Daniels and tells me he's owed €10,000 by some dodgy firm. I feel sorry for him, but I've heard this story before. Several times. So I listen, *uh-huh*, with one eye on the footy. After a respectful silence for Andy's lost dosh, I ask him if Leicester City could win the Premiership. Andy ignores the question and downs his Jack. He orders a draught beer from an eager young barman, and watches the oversized, foaming head rise inside the glass.

"They call that a *pint?* Typical. Romania drives me mad, Mick, useless place. Scams at the airport, scams at the exchange house, scams on contracts. Jesus, I just want to build decent stuff and make a bit of money for my trouble. But all I get is trouble."

"Invest in Leicester City, they're on a roll this season, see?"

He glances at the TV. "Fuck the Foxes."

The game ends, I pay for my apple juice, and Andy decides to leave with me. He doesn't pay anything before we go, even though he's had several drinks, just like last time. We walk side by side, along a cobbled street.

"How come you never pay, Andy?"

He sucks on a cigarette. "Got a tab running, is why." He blows smoke, with a wink. "Bar manager trusts me." Andy flags a cab. "Did I tell you about the taxi scam?"

Yes, Andy, goodbye, Andy.

Two weeks later, I return to Brașov to watch a big European game, but a storm is raging over the city and the TV screen is a swirling sea of white dots. Cezar the bar manager keeps apologising as if bad weather is his fault. He pushes his floppy fringe aside, but it won't stay put. Perhaps he should cut it off. He could use some sun, too. That nightclubber's tan makes him as pale as a wraith. Old before his time, is Cezar. Thirty-five going on fifty?

"Yo, dude," he says, towards the door.

Let me guess.

Andy waddles up to the bar, wearing a soggy raincoat and looking like he slept in a JCB. I'm looking pleased to see him. He slides his sizeable arse onto a seat, orders a draught beer, and drones on about the deluge outside. But soon enough, sure enough, he's back on message with his favourite theme.

"Mick, this country is one big scam. For example, did you watch that local footy match the other night? I did, at this dive in Bacău, *Hotel Cockroach*. What a game. Someone bribed the ref, I swear, what a fix. I tell you what, this place drives me mad."

"You don't say. How about United's new manager?"

"Van Gaal is a tosser and he'd better win us some silverware or he's out."

We stare at the screen on the wall.

"What are we watching, *Blizzard TV?*" says Andy – his best line for a while.

We sit chatting, or rather, I sit listening while he sips draught lager and rants about dodgy Romanian judges. I glance around at happy couples and lads thumbing phones. I'm ready to head home, but I don't fancy driving in a thunderstorm.

Andy beckons the anaemic bar manager. Cezar glides up and Andy leans across black marble, speaking in a low voice. "So, me old mate, what's me tab?"

"Wait, while I check." Cezar darts away and back again. "Let's call it seventy-five lei."

Andy offers a folded banknote. "Call it fifty, how's that?"

Cezar palms the cash into a pocket – *now you see it, now you don't* – then moves on to serve another customer. But something doesn't add up. The maths, for a start.

Andy seems to read my thoughts. "Problem, Mick?"

"Cheap drinks, for you."

Andy moves closer for a quiet word. "Mick, since you mention it, here's the thing. If Cezar prints a bill, it goes through the books, but this way, the tab doesn't. So, yeah, cheap booze for me and a decent tip for my man. Win-win. Cheers."

He sips lager, eyes closed. I should have guessed. Actually, I think I did.

"So, that's why you order draught, Andy?"

"What are you now, a fucking barman?"

"I was, yes, for several years."

"Then you should know the score."

"I know enough."

"I bet you can pull a pint, too. Ever watched these clowns?"

"I've watched them try. They're not pulling, though. It's all buttons, these days. If you want a proper pint, go to a proper pub."

"Back in Blighty, aye, don't tempt me."

"The Irish joint up the road sells decent draught Guinness."

"Tastes like fucking Marmite. I'm a lager man, Mick."

"I noticed. And these lads waste a lot of it."

"Which means Cezar can write mine off as spillage."

"Thought so."

"Who's counting, except you?" Andy smiles. He looks different somehow, warm and knowing, like a savvy uncle, which makes me realise Uncle Andy doesn't smile often. On the other hand, Cezar smiles a lot. He knows the score. I hope the brewery doesn't. They'll have his fringe.

"So, Andy, was the bar tab your idea or Cezar's?"

"Can't remember. Who cares? All I know is, I forgot my wallet one time. Couldn't pay. It was an accident, swear to God."

"But a convenient one."

"That's how it works, Mick, I did not invent the system."

Moments ago, it was an accident. Now it's a system. Andy shrugs, patting his pockets. Probably dying for a smoke, but rules is rules, even in Romania these days. Strange but true.

Andy sighs. "Besides, Cezar earns what, 300 euros a month, take home?"

"He's also risking his future, Andy."

"Mick, give me a break, I'm trying to do the guy a favour."

"Sure, but if Cezar gets caught, he'll need more than a favour. He'll need a new job."

"That's his problem. I've got enough to worry about. Van Gaal, for starters. And so have you. Liverpool are crap, these days."

We sit in silence, staring at the fuzzy screen. He's right. The season is half over and Leicester City are still top. Imagine that, underdogs win the league. Under*foxes*, to be fair.

"Who do you fancy in Romania, Andy? Steaua Bucharest?"

"Couldn't give a shit, I told you, Romanian footy is fixed. I fancy the women, full stop. It's about the only thing that keeps me here. Otherwise, I'd probably leave. Place is a fucking nightmare. Endless bureaucracy. Backhanders left and fucking right. I tell you what, business is one big game. Ten grand, I'm owed. Who makes the rules, eh?"

It's a difficult question, but I have an answer, sort of.

"I think you should stay, Andy."

"Why?"

"Because you're smart, and one day you'll figure out the rules of the game. See how things work. Then you'll clean up."

Andy looks almost happy until he looks back at the TV. Still no image. I glance away, through a window, at the glistening, bumpy streets of Brașov, where rain swirls like silver curtains opening and closing. Andy summons a junior barman and jabs a finger at the screen.

"Mate, do me a favour? Look at your television. It's fucking *snowing* in there. I buy drinks, I pay your wages, and I can't watch the fucking match. Call this a sports bar?"

Andy shoots me a look. Perhaps he's taking the piss, but the young barman is shitting bricks; he grabs the remote control, thumbs buttons, turns it the other way round, and thumbs more buttons. He casts it aside and pokes at the satellite receiver's console. *Poke, poke.* Still no good. He turns back to us, ashen-faced. "Domnul Andy, it's the storm, it's the service provider, it's—"

Andy groans. "Yeah, right, it's always someone fucking else."

Solomon the Wise Guy

Our big white sheepdog is a bit of a skellington and his wounds will take a while to heal, but he settles in soon enough and seems to enjoy his new home, hobbling around our yard and getting his polar bearings. Life can't be easy with twenty-five stitches in your scabby hide. He was in a fight, or something. Perhaps a shepherd beat him up. We'll probably never know.

As for a name, *Fleabag* won't do, because this dog has no fleas. His thick coat was just matted and mucky and now it's all clipped off. He looks like a shorn sheep. Perhaps we should call him *Sean Sheepdog*. Perhaps not; the other dogs will laugh.

"Hey, big boy, what's your name?" I crouch down but he won't say. His lovely brown eyes gaze back, through tufts of white hair. *Guess.* We try the obvious ones: *Bobiță, Ursulică,* and so on. No response.

Eventually, we decide to call him *Solomon* because he's quite old – about nine according to Cosmin the vet – and looks rather wise with that fluffy white beard.

"Hello, Solomon," I say and he gazes back. *Who's Solomon?*

At dinner time, however, I call him *You Vicious Greedy Bastard*, because he wants our dogs' food as well as his own and lunges for their throats if they get in his way.

"He's used to competition," says Angela.

"You're right. No wonder he got in a fight."

Needless to say, our other dogs Linda and Sam are scared poo-less every munch-time because bully-boy eats like two horses and is soon as strong as the ox down the road. But time heals all and, after a few weeks, Vicious Greedy Bastard realises there is plenty of grub to go around. No need to fight about it. He stops attacking our girlies and they all become best pals. *Wag-wag, nuzzle nuzzle.*

Linda and Sam teach Solomon who to bark at and when. For example, at anybody, any time, but especially in the early hours, right under our bedroom window. Howling can also be fun, preferably three-part harmonies: *Oo-oo-ow!* That's the bad news. The good news is, Solomon proves remarkably benign towards our five cats and enjoys sniffing their postal codes. *Hmm, nice.*

Our neighbours stare, the first time we take our decrepit new dog for walkies, because he's still covered in purple smudges. *What sort of dog is that,* they ask. We tell them he's a lucky one.

Local shepherds seem especially curious and keen to advise us, *He's a Mioritic, a real sheepdog.* They ponder Solomon's impressive injuries and posit explanations. Solomon barks ferociously until the shepherds back off. He knows something we don't.

The leaves curl and fall; our long hot summer cools into autumn. We build Solomon a stout wooden kennel with insulated walls and a raised floor for air to circulate below. I toss in plenty of sweet-smelling dry grass. He seems happy inside.

Come winter, Angela adds a nice woollen blanket. Next morning, we find it outside. Covered in snow. Solomon must have dragged it there. I peep in at his door and ask why. Big brown eyes glint at me through the gloom. *I'm a sheepdog, not a pussy cat.*

Sure enough, his scratchy patchy coat grows thick, his purple spots fade, and our friends urge us to post his photo on Facebook, *Because he's so handsome.* Solomon might concur but we don't, in case some shepherd comes to reclaim the dog that he loved so much, he severed its ear as a pup. No chance. Solomon is ours. He's a big, wise dog. He's fluffy and strong. He's cute and loud. In fact, there's only one thing Solomon isn't: obedient.

Ask him to do something, such as *Come back, you bugger* after he's escaped from the yard, and he'll just keep running. To catch him, you have to run as well. In your heavy winter boots. As fast as you can. Across the village. On snow and ice. Falling on your bottom. Up hill and down slalom course. For three kilometres. Until he stops for a number two. Then you grab his lead and say, *Who's a bad boy?* Solomon doesn't answer; he just blinks. Talk about gratitude. He probably thinks he's clever. After all, you can't teach an old dog new tricks. In fact, you can't teach it anything. Oh well, he's probably had a hard life and little TLC until now. So, we forgive his sins and love him as one of our own, which is what he's become.

By February, snowdrifts lie a metre deep across our yard and the dogs huddle in their kennels, bored stiff. I boil three big bones as treats to cheer them up. Needless to say, Solomon the wise guy has other ideas.

He comes running when I bring out the bones. He seizes the biggest and trots around with it in his jaws: *Look what I got.* So far, so good. I go back indoors and watch from a window, happy that he's happy. *When was the last time someone gave him a bone?* Bon appétit, Solomon. Or *poftă bună,* as we say in Romania.

But Solomon does not chew his bone. Instead, he walks about as if wondering what to do with it. On the slope below our vegetable patch, he digs a deep hole, drops the bone inside, and nudges snow on top. He spends a good five minutes at his task.

"Not hungry, perhaps," says Angela.

"I reckon he's up to something."

"What makes you think so?"

"Just a hunch, let's wait and see."

We watch Solomon trot towards our dog Linda. She's big and somewhat butch, but he's bigger and badder. He circles, sniffing the air, eyeing her bone. Linda growls and snaps a warning: *Back off.* Solomon moves on to Sam. She's gnawing her bone. She's snappy, too, but considerably smaller than Solomon. He's watching and waiting for his chance; it comes soon enough.

A donkey ambles down the lane beyond our fence, hauling a large sled containing a neighbour and two rocking milk churns. Sam abandons her bone and goes to investigate, *yap-yap.* Solomon clamps his jaws on the discarded bone. *Gotcha.* He trots away.

I turn to my wife. "See that? Just as I thought."

"Dog eat dog, I suppose. Not much we can do."

"Perhaps I can teach him a lesson."

"How?"

"Watch."

I take a walking stick from the lobby and leave the house. The donkey has gone and Sam is curled in her kennel, looking miserable. She watches Solomon chewing her bone. *Sly bastard.*

I summon Sam to follow me down to the spot where Solomon buried his bone, earlier. She follows, wagging her tail, curious.

I poke my stick in the snow, trying to find the bone. No luck. I kneel and dig with my hands. Sam gets the scent, joins in, and we find it. I carry the bone up the slope and onto our terrace. Sam follows, her tail flicking. I lock the terrace gate behind us and she settles down to chew Solomon's bone, in peace. *Justice.*

Angela and I stand sipping tea, nibbling biscuits, and looking into the wide valley below. It sparkles white with snow.

Sam stares at us from the terrace. Her bone lies nearby, denuded of meat. She would scoot indoors if invited. I shake my head.

"This is not a doggy place."

"I wonder where Solomon is?" says Angela.

We spot him soon enough. He's below the vegetable patch, digging frantically in the snow. He pauses to look up, gobbets of ice clinging to his face. His stumpy ear looks like a lost sock and his nose is a chunk of shiny coal. But those eyes. So intelligent. So knowing. Solomon gazes at me, like on the day we met for the first time. But today he's asking a different question.

Who's been in my flipping fridge?

One Way

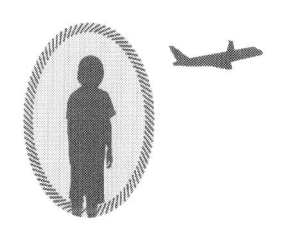

Angela sounds wary, but, as ever, willing to help. She ends the phone call and says, "How odd. That was Doamna Jeni from up the lane. She wants to discuss something personal, face-to-face. Needs my advice, as soon as possible, it seems. Wouldn't tell me what about, but she'll be here in ten minutes."

"Silent Jeni phoned you? Imagine that. Must be important."

"Apparently it is and she wants privacy. Can't even discuss it on the phone."

I turn a page in my book. "The plot thickens. Wonder why not."

"She's at home and doesn't want her parents listening in," says Angela. "They share that tiny cottage. Walls have ears, I guess."

"Not to mention her kids; little Rafael can be a right chatterbox."

"Actually, Jeni's bringing him here, and her daughter Simona, too."

I look up and Angela shrugs. Bang goes our quiet afternoon.

The young, single mum arrives by car, forty-five minutes late. Jeni is pretty, petite, and timorous, wearing a beige faux-leather bomber jacket, tight beige jeans, slinky beige boots, and beige lipstick. Her hair is a neat bob and dyed mauve. A beige bag dangles from a dainty wrist. Her two children hop from the back of her little red Dacia, but I wonder why she drove it here, as we're only a three-minute walk. *In those heels, along our potholed lane?* Maybe not.

Blond-haired Rafael stares at me through our fence. He's only five years old, but you cross him at your peril. His sister, eight-year-old Simona carries a posy of wildflowers – perhaps for Doamna Angela. Nice gesture, if so. *But so much for Jeni's privacy.*

Here they come, through the gate, up the steps, and into the house. For a noisy young family who think nothing of blasting *manele* music from a huge speaker on their doorstep, Jeni & company seem oddly subdued today. Perhaps the speaker blew up. That would certainly stop their neighbours complaining.

Angela puts the flowers in a vase – *mulțumesc* – and invites our guests to sit around the dining table. They settle in silence – even mercurial Rafael seems well-behaved. *How come?* He's wearing an oversized, purple sweatshirt with an embroidered logo: *Thorpe Willoughby Childcare Centre.* Jeni found it in a second-hand shop, probably. Seems to be working, wherever it came from.

Simona wears green floral leggings, a green checked shirt, and a green hairband. Even her fingernails are painted green. No bag, though; just bags of style, like *Mama.*

I serve the kids glasses of cherry juice and they say, *mulțumesc*. I serve Jeni some and she says, "Have you got a computer?"

"Sure," says Angela, fetching her laptop.

The ladies have work to do. Something, anyway. Me too.

"I'll be in my study if you need me, Angela. Catch you later, Jeni."

Jeni gazes up at me, doe-eyed. She looks troubled, miles away.

"Domnul Mike."

"Yes, Rafael?"

"What are you doing in here?"

"I'm working, what are you doing in here?"

"Nothing." He caresses the strings on one of my guitars, back and forth, *twaa-ang*. "When are you going to teach me ukulele?"

"Perhaps when you're a little older, Rafael. It didn't go so well the last time we tried, remember?"

Rafael sits on my sofa, looking around the room. "Uh-huh."

"Bored?" I ask.

He nods, so I rise from my chair. "Come with me."

We sit cross-legged on the floor, around the coffee table, in the lounge at the back of the house. Rafael says *I've done this giraffe puzzle before,* but it doesn't look like it. More like a snake, in fact.

Simona edges closer. "You're supposed to put the numbered blocks in the correct sequence, that's how you get a giraffe."

"Don't want a giraffe," says Rafael, which is just as well.

"Have fun," I tell them. "Look in our books, too, if you like pictures. All sorts here, from museums and galleries, see?"

The kids ignore me and huddle over the puzzle.

Back at the dining table, Angela tells me that Jeni wants to leave.

"Fair enough," I say, "nice to see you, Doamna Jeni. I'll go and tell your kids."

Angela taps at her keyboard. "I mean, Jeni wants to leave Culmea. She wants to leave Romania, for good. Next week. That's why she came to see me."

News indeed. I join them at the table. "Leave Culmea, Jeni? Leave *Romania?*"

She shrugs. "Had enough, Domnul Mike."

"Of?"

"My parents. This village. This country. Everything." She stares at her empty glass. Enough said. She's made her decision.

Angela points at her laptop. "So, I've found a Thursday flight to Gatwick for you, 200 euros. Wizz Air, return. That's not bad, Jeni."

Jeni shakes her mauve bob, *swish-swish.* "One-way ticket, I want."

Angela looks at me. We both look at Jeni. I reckon it's probably time for a you-know-what.

"Cup of tea, anyone?"

"Like in England," says Jeni, with a lop-sided smile.

Over a welcome cuppa, Jeni tells us she'll travel to the UK as soon as Culmea's village school closes for the summer holidays, so her kids can finish their classes and the teachers won't accuse her of abandoning her job.

"Some job," says Jeni, "I'm sick of cleaning that place for 800 lei."

I dip a biscuit in my tea, converting currency in my head. *200 euros per month?* That doesn't go far, especially with two kids.

"So, you're taking Rafael and Simona to England?" I ask.

Jeni makes a face, *as if.*

"They'll stay in Culmea?" I say.

"No, Domnul Mike. I'll move them down to Dumbrăvița, to stay with their dad. They like being with him and it's about time he learned what it means to raise our kids, day in, day out. He's got a full-time job but he'll find a way. Like I had to, all these years."

"Why not leave Simona and Rafael in Culmea with their grandparents?" Angela asks.

"Because my parents refused to look after them, if I go abroad."

"Your parents *refused?*"

Jeni nods. "I'm sick of them. I get no help. All I get is grief. You know why? Boyfriends. The first one, they blocked him, two years ago. They told me, *End it or else.* So, I did. Eventually, I met another fellow. I wasn't looking for anyone, of course, not after all that nastiness, but, well, you know how it is. Bogdan came as a tourist from Bucharest one weekend. He bought some of my cow's milk, and we got chatting. Then, guess what."

"Blocked?" say Angela.

"Yup, and God knows why. Actually, tell a lie, I do know why. My Dad told me, *God sees everything.* So, I told him, *God should mind his own business.* Mama didn't like that and Tata threatened me with his blackthorn stick. Mama gets palpitations, from me, she said. I said I get nothing from her, just grief. Then we had a row."

"Because you're still seeing this Bogdan fellow from Bucharest?"

"Yes, Domnul Mike, except now he's in London, that's why I want to go. I can get a job. I don't care what. There are vacancies, in the vacancy place, for better money. I'll do whatever's going. I've worked in this village, on my knees in mud and cow shit, in all weather, for years. And cleaning the school. So, I don't mind work, especially if it pays better. Bogdan told me, *London's the place.* Or Melbourne."

"Australia, really?"

"That's where it is, yes. His children live there, you see. Son and daughter, same as I've got. Quite a coincidence, no? Marius owns a garage and Mirela works in an office. I've got photos."

I look at Angela, and she says, "Jeni, how old is Bogdan?"

"Fifty-six. I'm thirty-five. That's another reason, of course."

"For?"

"Why my folks won't look after the kids if I go. *Shame on you,* and all that. I told Bogdan what they said, but he told me to come, even so. And I'll go, if I can afford a ticket. I've never been on a plane so I'm bit scared, but I have to be brave. I'm finished with Culmea."

Jeni sits back and sighs. What a speech. I'm speechless. In the seven years I've known her, she's hardly said three words to me. Now this? No wonder little Rafael can yap, when it suits him. And no wonder he's so determined, at times, just like Mama. But something is amiss in her plan. Angela's spotted it too, I think.

"Jeni, a return ticket costs more but is a safer option," she says.

"Especially if your kids are staying here," I add.

"And then there's Brexit, of course," says Angela.

"Can't Bogdan help out with your fare?" I ask.

Jeni's little beige lips pucker into a pout, while she considers her reply.

"No, but he sent me a screenshot."

"A screenshot?"

"I showed it to Doamna Angela, wait."

Jeni thumbs her phone and holds it up for me to see. *WizzAir.* She flicks her mauve fringe and tilts her head, smiling sweetly, as if practising for the day she'll approach the Immigration booth.

Back in our lounge, my alphabetical giraffe puzzle looks like a tapeworm in need of a host.

Rafael sits grinning at me. "I did it."

"You certainly did, Rafael. What is it?"

"A puzzle."

"I'll say."

Simona doesn't say much. She's flicking through our big book about The Louvre. She reaches the classical sculpture section and says, "Wow." Rafael has a peep and titters at the marble nudes.

I slide into an armchair. "So, I hear you guys are moving to Dumbrăvița?"

Simona nods, po-faced and preoccupied. "Uh-huh."

Rafael grins. "And Mama's going to London."

"I know, Rafael, she just told me. London, eh? Imagine that."

"But don't tell anyone else, Domnul Mike. We have to be quiet for a bit, especially me."

"I won't say a word. Maybe you'll go there too, some day?"

"Maybe," says Simona, turning glossy pages.

She'd prefer Paris, by the sound of it. She shoves the book aside, with a sigh. *Maybe not.* She glances about, left and right, chewing her bottom lip just like Mama. She rises to her feet and beckons Rafael, pointing at something more interesting, beyond my sight.

Sunshine floods the lounge. The big windows flash and sparkle. It's too hot back here, and the golden light is so bright, you can hardly see anything except for a million specks of dust, all floaty.

The children creep around the lounge, two silhouettes tiptoeing past my armchair, looking here and there and whispering to each other, as they explore the possibilities of a new place.

Author Bio

Mike Ormsby was born in Ormskirk, England. His short story collection, *Never Mind the Balkans, Here's Romania* (2008), prompted Romanian critics to dub him "our British Caragiale", after their beloved Victorian-era satirist.

Mike is the author of *Child Witch Kinshasa* and *Child Witch London* (2014), a two-part novel set in Congo and the UK. *Spinner the Winner* (2012), his book for children, has been translated into French, Serbian, Spanish and Romanian. His screenplay *Hey, Mr. DJ* (2007) was filmed in Kigali and shown at Rwanda's first Hillywood Film Festival.

A former BBC journalist/World Service trainer, Mike is based in a village in Transylvania, where he and his wife Angela Nicoară have lived for five hundred years.

DON'T MISS

MIKE ORMSBY'S
NEVER MIND THE VAMPIRES HERE'S TRANSYLVANIA

After twenty years of living in cities around the world, British writer Mike Ormsby settles in a tiny village in Romania's fabled Transylvania, where the air is clean, the scenery spectacular, and solitude a balm for the soul. Well, sort of. Mike and his wife Angela soon discover that their learning curve is as steep as a Carpathian slope. Join them in Transylvania! And never mind the vampires.

Gives an absolutely spot-on sense of rural life in a changing Transylvania, with cutting insights and a wry sense of humour.
Tim Burford, Author, *The Rough Guide to Romania*

Poignant, immediate, always original. Ormsby is the perfect guide.
Robin Ashenden, *Central and Eastern European London Review*

Ormsby addresses rural Romania with a deep understanding, wit, a zeal for storytelling, a poetic sense of what is right, and a profound respect.
Colin Shaw, Founder & Tour Guide, *Roving Romania*

The modern world is turning rural Romania upside down and inside out. Mike Ormsby captures well the agony and ecstasy of this transition.
William Blacker, Author, *Along The Enchanted Way*

An excellent blend of dialogue, wit, and subtle irony.
Dr. Gabriela Colipca-Ciobanu, Associate Professor, Dunărea de Jos University

Ormsby's gift appears to be his willingness to talk to people, find things out and deal with any situation, no matter how ridiculous. Sublime.
Craig Turp, Editor, *Bucharest in Your Pocket*

EXCERPT OVERLEAF

SAMPLE

NEVER MIND THE VAMPIRES HERE'S TRANSYLVANIA

MIKE ORMSBY

The Lovely Linda

"You're back with us in Bucharest, Domnul Mike?" The cleaning lady waddles towards me in the lobby of the apartment block, pushing her trolley of buckets and brushes. Her flip-flops slap a welcome on the tiles as she approaches. "Did you press the button for the lift?"

"Yes, Doamna Tina, it should be here soon. How are you?"

"Not bad, thanks for asking. How's Doamna Angela?"

"Fine, thanks. She's upstairs in our flat."

We step into the lift and Tina pokes the control panel. She looks tired and much older than the last time we met. *Just over four years ago?* Her hands are pale, almost transparent. Must be all those buckets of soapy water. She reaches out to steady a nervous mop.

"So, where are you these days, Domnul Mike?"

"Azerbaijan, until last week. We just moved back to Romania. How are things in the block?"

"Same as ever, here."

We rise through the floors and an awkward silence descends. Nothing like a small elevator for accentuating big differences. I stare at the stainless steel door and spot a familiar graffito gouged into it: *Suck me, Vlaicu.*

It's still here after all these years. So much for our esteemed Administrator, but that's democracy, I suppose.

"How long are you two staying in Bucharest?" says Tina.

"Not long, we're moving to Transylvania. Bought a house."

"Oh, I see. So, that means you'll have a garden?"

"Quite a big one."

"Then why not take Linda?"

"Linda who?"

"Linda who lives in the car park."

"I beg your pardon?"

"Linda's a dog. Look." Tina pulls out her scuffed Nokia and shows me a photo of a scary dog with a black face and stern gaze. "She's a beauty, Domnul. See how alert! Make a good guard dog. Her dad was a Rottweiler. You'll need a dog. Do you have one?"

"No, although we are thinking about it. I want a local sheepdog, a *Ciobănesc* with a thick coat for the cold winters."

"You should take Linda, everybody here loves her."

"In that case, why has nobody here adopted her?"

"Linda's too big for these little flats, she needs to be outside."

The bell pings and the elevator doors slide apart. Tina spots Angela stacking cardboard boxes in the corridor beyond and steps out with me. She gives my wife a welcoming hug and tells her about lovely Linda who lives in the car park and why we must adopt her.

Angela checks the photo. "Linda looks a bit fierce, Tina."

"Doamna Angela, trust me, she's a lovely dog. I'll take you to meet her if you like. But the sooner the better." Tina sounds sad.

"How do you mean?" says Angela.

"The dogcatchers took her. They'll kill her, any day now."

"Kill Linda?"

"At the compound, it's what they do. Won't you save her?"

Angela looks at me and we know the answer. *Bang goes my sheepdog.*

"Are you free to visit the compound tomorrow?" says Angela.

Tina wipes tearful eyes on a sleeve. "I'll take time off."

"Great, thanks, Tina. We'll go by taxi. Say, 9 a.m.?"

"Actually, I know a lady who might drive us."

"Even better."

Nine sharp, Tina is waiting for us in the car park, dressed in a long grey anorak over a summer frock and red sandals. A skinny blonde stands nearby smoking a long cigarette and wearing a black trouser suit, black beret, silky green scarf, and big sunglasses. She looks French, as in *Résistance*. What she doesn't look is happy. Tina introduces her. "This is my friend Madeleine. She'll drive us to the dog pound."

Turns out *La Madeleine* lives in the next block, loves animals, and has rescued six street cats, some of whom appear to have slept on her beret. She jangles car keys above her head. "Borrowed some wheels. Shall we?" She beckons us and we obey, somewhat intrigued.

"Catchers can be such horrible people," says Madeleine, striding on. "They just grab any dog they can, doesn't matter what you say. I also rescued four terriers from this car park. They live on my land outside

Bucharest. I would take Linda but she's too big. I hope she's still alive. I dread going to the compound, it's terribly upsetting, I usually cry my eyes out. But any friend of Tina's is a friend of mine." She glances at the sky and frowns. "Looks like rain. Here's the car. Hop in."

The first raindrops patter down as Angela and I squeeze into a white Dacia. It's nice to be rescued. *A good omen?*

Madeleine removes her sunglasses and looks at us in the rear-view mirror. Her green eyes match her scarf, très chic.

"Listen up, guys. I can't promise anything except that we'll try, ок? Linda's quite nice-looking, so chances are she's still alive."

"They don't euthanize nice-looking dogs?" says Angela.

Madeleine smiles at us for the first time. "No, they sell 'em, even though adoptions are supposed to be free. Let's go!"

She's a good driver – not too fast, not too slow, checking her mirrors and keeping her distance. The rain is torrential and our windows are all foggy.

The dog pound consists of a few single-storey concrete buildings and a big yard behind a steel fence. We park nearby but remain in the car, waiting for the rain to ease off. We should've brought umbrellas.

"Mind if I smoke?" says Madeleine.

"Yes," says Tina.

"Shall we phone and say we've come for Linda?" says Angela.

"No point," says Madeleine, "they won't have a clue who you mean, they have far too many dogs."

"Not like Linda, they don't," says Tina. "She's lovely, she's not some mutt, like that one." Tina points at some mutt in the yard.

"Lovely unless you're a cat," says Madeleine. "Linda hates cats."

Angela glances at me. "Hear that? Linda hates cats."

"I heard. We should get a puppy instead. Sheepdog puppy."

Madeleine looks at us in the mirror. "Is there a problem?"

"Yes, we have four cats in our flat, back at the block."

"Since when did you have cats in your flat?" says Tina.

"We brought them last week from Azerbaijan, we rescued them a while ago."

Madeleine stares at Tina. *"Four cats?* You didn't say they had cats. I'm wasting my time. They can't adopt Linda, she'll eat the lot."

"I never saw Linda eat one, she just chases them," says Tina.

I lean forward. "Tina, if Linda hates cats we can't adopt her."

"She doesn't hate them, she just chases them for fun."

"It's not fun if you're a cat. What if she catches one of ours?"

"I never saw her catch one. They usually run up trees and hiss."

"We don't have trees in our apartment."

"But you're moving to Transylvania. *Quite a big garden,* you said. Oh, look, the rain's stopping. We can go and find Linda."

I sit back, wondering whether to stay put. Tina the cleaner would make a good chess player, I reckon, always one move ahead. And she's right about the rain – the deluge is drying up, just a few silver plops bouncing here and there. But she's wrong if she thinks we're adopting a cat killer.

Madeleine opens her door. "Whatever, let's try while we can."

"Well, Mike?" says Angela.

I shrug my shoulders. *Whatever.* We exit the car and follow our guides, dodging wisps of cigarette smoke. The sky rumbles, sunshine cracks a cloud, and puddles shimmer petrol blue.

Inside the main building, we stand around waiting to speak to a burly official behind the counter. He has a bushy, grey beard and horn-rimmed spectacles. He's barking into a phone. Perhaps he's worked here too long. We look at maps of Bucharest pinned on a wall. Coloured bits show where the dogcatchers have been, and when. Tina points to Sector 5.

"Here's our street, Domnul Mike."

"I know."

The telephone clatters into its cradle and Greybeard spreads his arms, gripping the counter. His body language says, *Stay away,* but he says, "How can I help?"

Tina explains, Madeleine explains, then Greybeard explains.

"What the hell. The dog you want is probably dead by now. *Three weeks,* you say? Why didn't you come sooner?" He scratches his beard. It's hard work dealing with idiots. Or perhaps he's got fleas.

"Could you at least check if Linda's still here?" says Tina. "She's nice-looking. Black and brown. Sort of a Rottweiler."

"*Sort of a Rottweiler?* It doesn't matter what sort. Two weeks and we zap 'em. That's the rule. You should've come sooner."

Angela steps forward. "Excuse me, sir, but these ladies didn't try sooner because they can't adopt a dog like Linda. Because they live in small flats and adopted several dogs already. However, my husband and I can adopt a dog. We arrived in Romania two days ago and came here as soon as we could. We're simply asking you to check if Linda is still alive, that's all."

Greybeard seems surprised. "I see. Where did you come from?"

"Azerbaijan."

"So, why didn't you adopt a dog there?"

"Please, sir."

He sighs. "Very well, walk this way. And only you. Not this lot."

"Better if you take Tina or Madeleine. They know the dog."

"Suit yourself, but I haven't got all day."

Madeleine nudges Tina – *you go* – and Tina follows Greybeard.

They return ten minutes later. Tina looks fed up. Madeleine grabs her by the arm.

"Did you find Linda?"

"Not sure. There's one dog that looks like her. Sitting alone. Scared and skinny. I can't tell. I called her name, but–"

Madeleine turns to Greybeard. "May I check, too?"

He gawps at Angela. "Jesus, how long is this going to take?"

"Sir, please let Madeleine try?"

"What, you couldn't find any stray dogs in Afghanistan?"

"We're only trying to help." Tina blows her nose into a hanky.

Greybeard looks ready to blow a fuse. "Yes, of course you are."

He marches out, beckoning Madeleine. I look again at the coloured map on the wall. It represents a modern solution to an old problem, and makes me wonder. *What if Ceaușescu had not forced his citizens to live in tiny apartments, during Romania's so-called Golden Era?* They wouldn't have abandoned their dogs, is what. But he did, and they did, and now look. A map of Bucharest, bright as a rainbow. But it doesn't end in a pot of gold. It ends here, in a concrete yard enclosed by a fence, then with a needle in the arse.

Greybeard returns soon enough, with Madeleine. She can barely speak for weeping. She hugs Tina. "Yes, it's Linda, she's alive!"

"Great, so we can adopt her," says Angela.

"No," says Greybeard, "someone already did, two days ago."

"Pardon?"

"Like I said, that big black one is already adopted." Greybeard walks to a little window in the wall behind him. He slides it back and murmurs to a younger, elfin-faced fellow in the office beyond. The elf smiles at us through the glass. He has short, sticky-up hair, shirt and tie, and an agreeable air. One of life's optimists, I reckon, for whom the stray dog pound is always half-empty. Greybeard returns to the counter and gives a little cough, shuffling papers. He seems to have forgotten all about us.

"If Linda has been adopted," says Angela, "why is she still here?"

Greybeard doesn't even look up. "Why are you still here?"

"We won't leave until you answer the question," I say.

"Very well. The dog is here because the people who adopted it are coming back."

"When?"

"One of these days."

"Perhaps they changed their mind. Could you phone them?"

"No time for that."

"What about your young colleague, next door?"

"Costel is busy, no time."

"We've got time. Could you give us their number, please?"

"Confidential." Greybeard flicks documents, busy being busy. "Come tomorrow and see if that dog is still here. Good day."

Angela plants her elbows on his counter. "It takes us an hour to get here. It would take two minutes to phone those people."

"Sorry, I can't help you."

Madeleine is sobbing quietly into a fist, but that won't help either. Tina caresses her shoulder. "Wasting our time, Maddy."

We troop out, single file, in silence. We're halfway across the car park when a voice calls out, somewhere behind us. "Doamna, stop!"

We stop. Young Costel with the sticky-up hair scoots across glistening tarmac and says to Angela, "You want to see Linda?"

"What's the point? She's been adopted. Apparently."

"Even so, you want to see her? Domnul, how about you?"

"That's why we came, but what difference will it make?"

"Just come, follow me!"

We glance at Tina and Madeleine – *whatever* – and follow Costel towards the yard, where dogs of all shapes and sizes are emerging from cages to yawn, stretch, and lap at puddles. Some bark at us and trot up and down, behind the wire fence. They seem excited rather than aggressive. Madeleine cups a hand to her mouth.

"Linda!"

A large, skinny dog looks up. Madeleine shouts again. The dog bounds forward and stands on hind legs at the fence, whining. Tina reaches through to ruffle brown ears. "Linda, my beauty!"

Linda might have been a beauty once, but no longer. Her ribs and vertebrae are visible and her black coat is patchy. Yes, she's good-looking, keen-eyed, friendly, and seems intelligent, but she's not for us. Even if we could adopt this fierce-looking wretch, she'd freeze in the first Transylvanian winter. Linda is a city dog and already adopted. *So why are we playing lovey-dovey through a fence?* Costel nudges my arm. "This is Linda, isn't it, Domnul?"

"Seems so."

He nudges me again. "And you like her, yes?"

"I'm just glad she'll have a home. Got any fluffy sheepdogs?"

He gives me a wolfish grin. "No, they live in the mountains."

"Never mind. Thanks anyway. Bye Linda. Let's go, Angela."

We walk away, grim-faced, but Costel scurries after us, tugging at Angela's arm. *"Doamna, hai să facem să fie bine."*

Let's find a way, madam.

Angela turns, curious. "What did you say?"

Costel shrugs. "Let's make it OK for everyone. Follow me, please?"

He leads us back to the offices, but this time we enter through a rear door and stand in a corridor. Framed photos of happy dogs line the walls. Costel is smiling. We smile too, but I have no idea why. Perhaps he thinks we're telepathic. Luckily for him, Angela is.

"What, you want a bribe?" she says.

"As I said, let's find a way if you want to adopt Linda."

"Who's already been adopted," I suggest.

"Domnul, let's make everyone happy, including Linda."

"I thought dog adoptions in Romania are free?" says Angela.

"Yes, but let's try if you like."

"Incredible." Angela looks at me. "Well, Mike?"

"I'd say *yes*. She's quite a dog, but she'll freeze in mountains."

"She won't freeze, trust me," says our spiky-haired fixer.

Angela opens her purse. "Here's fifty lei, how's that?"

Costel raises his pixie chin and peeps into her purse.

"What, not enough?" I say, almost laughing. He just smiles.

243

Angela hands over another fifty. Costel slips the banknotes into a pocket. "This way, please."

Greybeard is busy with a foolscap folder, probably stuffed with money from fools like us. As we enter the reception area for the second time, he looks at Angela, then at his young colleague. His expression gives nothing away; here they give dogs away.

"You're back, Madam." It's not a question, more of a grunt.

"Yes, Linda is available after all. So, do I fill in a form?"

"No, as I said, come tomorrow for an update."

"An *update?* I just gave this guy a hundred lei. So, give me the dog."

Greybeard pulls a face. He seems baffled. "I don't follow."

"Oh, really?" says Angela, "what, you think we're stupid?"

"Stupid?" He pulls another face. From his repertoire.

Now it's my turn. "Give us the dog or give us our money."

"Domnul, adoptions are free."

"I want to speak to your supervisor," says Angela.

"Madam, fill in a complaint form and I'll look into it."

"You'll put it in your bin as soon as we leave."

"Madam, this is not Afghanistan, this is Romania."

"Where dog adoptions are free. Give me the money."

"What money?"

"And your names. For when I call my friends at Pro TV."

"Pro TV?"

Dogs bark in the distance. Our spiky-haired fixer coughs, and slinks away through a door.

Tina tugs Angela's arm. "Doamna Angela, Costel just gave me your money back."

"Creeps," says Madeleine, wiping her nose, "let's go."

"I'm very sorry," says Greybeard, "for any misunderstanding. Call us tomorrow, first thing. If you wish to adopt, bring a work contract and proof of residence. These are the rules. We have to be careful. There are some unscrupulous people out there."

"Not to mention in here," says Angela, and Madeleine laughs.

Trooping across the car park, we see no unscrupulous people. Just dogs locked in a compound.

"I'm done with this place," says Angela, "it's ridiculous."

"But, Doamna, what about poor Linda?" says Tina.

"We'll look for a poor sheepdog," I say, "in our village in Transylvania."

"Hmm, but when will you go, Domnul Mike?"

"By the end of this week we'll be there, *insha'Allah.*"

Tina looks confused. "I never heard of that place."

Our four cats from Azerbaijan couldn't care less about Linda or any other dog, I can tell. They curl on our balcony, snoozing in the midday sun. No rain today, lucky us. Traffic drones along the street below. Bucharest sounds just like Baku, but Transylvania will be different. Green and quiet. With a big, fluffy sheepdog. *Should I warn these lazy cats?* Nah, Angela can tell them when she gets off the phone. I wonder who called.

Angela joins me on the balcony. "That was Tina."

"And?"

"She's got the dog, she's got Linda."

"What?"

"She went back to the pound, this morning, with what's-her-name."

"Madeleine's going to adopt Linda?"

"No, *we* are. Madeleine filed the paperwork. Linda is at a clinic, she's washed and vaccinated. They gave her some vitamin shots. All we have to do is collect her. It's walking distance. Someone at the clinic will transfer ownership to us. To me, actually."

"You agreed to adopt Linda?"

"Why not?"

"You saw Linda's fur, she'll freeze."

"Linda will be fine in a kennel, no problem."

"Says who?"

"The vet at the clinic. Tina asked him. She's very helpful."

"She's a busybody. Linda hates cats. You'll regret this, I bet."

"We'll see. Oh, and we owe Tina fifty lei, don't let me forget."

"She had to pay for the clinic?"

"No, she had to pay those creeps at the dog pound."

"Where adoptions are free? What a scam."

"Look on the bright side, Linda's free."

"You can tell the cats. And mention the big garden."

"I will. Transylvania, here we come."

Red in Tooth and Claw

Radu has a farmer's tan, a lazy smile, and forearms that could throw me over his fence. He stands in his courtyard, sharpening a knife with a six-inch blade that glints in the morning sun. He thanks me for coming. I ask him how he feels about killing animals. He shrugs, glancing at distant mountains shrouded in pale grey mist.

"Did my first pig when I was ten. Difficult, that was, but not anymore. Come, you can help."

He walks to a gloomy shed and murmurs to a beautiful brown calf inside it. He nudges the timid animal into the sunny yard, wrestles it to the ground, trusses its hind legs together, and opens its neck with his blade. He rises without a word, and stands back. Job done.

The calf makes no sound. Blood flows and hooves kick. An inquisitive white cat prowls nearby; it sees what we're up to and probably knows that this brief carnage means a long feast, sooner or later. The calf stares at the cat with eyes that acquire a milky glaze as the minutes pass. I'm wondering what to say to Radu. His calm expertise is impressive, if that's the right word, but questions remain.

"Radu, why didn't you stun the calf?"

"Stun it? Too painful. Put it this way, how would you like a whack in the head with a hammer? Plus, a stun gun is too expensive. Anyway, time to skin this in the barn. Grab a leg."

We drag the dead calf across the grass, leaving a slimy, scarlet trail. Radu slings the rope around a crossbeam and we hoist the calf upside down, until it dangles a few inches above the ground. He pulls a Swiss Army penknife from his pocket and makes careful incisions in the carcass. *Cut and tug, cut and tug.* The hide gapes and drapes, freshly peeled. The farm cat approaches and crouches below the carcass, lapping at a pool of dark blood; its white head is soon spattered with red, as if painted by Jackson Pollock. *Vampire Puss*.

Radu is hacking gently at the hide. *Cut and tug, cut and tug*. It's tough work and he's breathing hard. "You like a bit of tasty veal, eh, Mike?" He has a mischievous twinkle in his eye, as so often. "Oh, sorry, I forgot. Vegetarian, right?"

"Right, Radu."

"Since when?"

"1982."

"1982? I wasn't even born." He stands back, pointing his blade at the carcass. "I need a rest. Want to try?"

"OK."

"Don't puncture the hide."

"What happens if I do?"

"I'll string you up by your ankles, is what." Radu gives me a gap-toothed smile, and his bloody penknife.

The carcass sways gently on its rope, like a punch bag. The sight of the bloodied beast reminds me of that line by Tennyson: *Nature, red in tooth and claw.* Oh well, here goes.

The exposed flesh is greyish pink and warm to the touch. Holding the knife in my right hand, I cut the skin, and tug at the hide with my left, wondering what I'm doing here. Radu folds his arms and watches me, as if wondering the same.

The answer is that we all need help sometimes, and today is my turn to help him, if that's what I'm doing. Because he's one of our neighbours and I owe him a favour or three. His bubbly wife Raluca often brings us eggs and cheese. That's how it is up here – they've been kind to us since we moved to the village a few months ago, and now we're friends, close to the land. Or trying to be, in my case, which is why I'm puzzled that Radu asked me to help slaughter a calf. Perhaps he's testing the newcomer with this *rite de passage*.

I lean closer, working the blade from left to right, across and down. *Don't puncture the hide.* It's hard to believe that this creature was alive and well, just a short while ago. What a way to die, poor thing. Then again, a flashing knife to the jugular vein is perhaps more humane and less stressful than a bumpy ride to some clanking abattoir reeking of stale blood. And Radu's probably right about that hammer. *No thanks.*

I do my best, but stand back after ten minutes to let Radu take over. He works quickly, removing the rest of the hide, then uses a bigger knife for butchering the carcass.

His impromptu biology lesson is grimly illuminating. I learn the location and function of the various internal organs, and how his wife will cook them. He shoves his forearm deep into the guts, extracts a translucent pouch and cuts it open to reveal a chalky deposit.

"We add this white stuff to our cheese."

249

I peep at the white stuff in the pouch. It's rennet, probably. It's certainly time for me to leave because this musty barn seems warmer by the minute and smells sickly sweet. The dead calf's head is in a bucket of crimson water and mine is in need of fresh air.

Never Mind the Vampires, Here's Transylvania
is available on *Amazon*